CRAYON SKETCHES

AND

Off-Hand Takings,

— OF —

DISTINGUISHED AMERICAN STATESMEN, ORATORS,
DIVINES, ESSAYISTS, EDITORS, POETS,
AND PHILANTHROPISTS.

BY

GEORGE W. BUNGAY.

Some are born great, some achieve greatness, —
And some have greatness thrust upon them.
SHAKSPEARE.

BOSTON:
Stacy and Richardson, Printers,
No. 11 Milk Street.

INTRODUCTION.

It was in the Spring of 1850 that the author of the following Sketches called, one day, into the office of the *New-Englander*, in Boston, (whither he was then much accustomed to resort,) and during a conversation which ensued with the editors of that sheet,—then somewhat known in this vicinity as a temperance, literary, and family journal,—the subject of the preparation of a series of articles on the prominent men of the day was discussed, and favorably entertained. The author's previous effusions had been marked with a good deal of pith and piquancy, and the conductors of the *New-Englander* considered that an highly interesting feature would be added to their paper by his regular contributions, written in the free and cordial manner which was his wont.

Nor were their expectations disappointed. Mr. Bungay's pursuits having, at different periods, brought him in connection with many of the leading men of our country,—possessing a mind unusually well refreshed with the thoughts of our best writers, both in prose and verse,—and, withal, being himself a man of earnest and kindly sympathies, he was in every respect qualified for the task he had assumed. It had been previously perceived, in Mr. Bungay's occasional newspaper effusions, that he was gifted more particularly with the power of terse, graphic, off-hand, sententious remark, than with that of elaborate description, or polished finish and ornament. This he himself acknowledged; and thus, by general consent, he styled his productions in this line, "OFF-HAND TAKINGS," and assumed the art-word of "CRAYON," as the most appropriate signature for one whose light and dark shades upon the pictures of his imagination were so agreeably diversified.

With a heart and a pride in the work, therefore, the author of the following Sketches entered upon his task; and to his credit, it must be said, he immediately won a popularity which many have envied, and but few attained. An increased demand for copies of the paper was quickly perceptible; contemporaneous journals, it was observed, freely copied his articles; and, in brief, all the customary indications were had that Mr. BUNGAY had made a successful essay in his projected enterprise, while the editors of the *New-Englander* became the recipients of many thanks for affording the medium through which he had thus successfully communicated with the public.

The following work contains nearly all the Sketches which appeared in the *New Englander*, a few others written more lately for different journals, and a still less number prepared expressly for this edition. Each has been carefully revised, all redundancy of language or thought omitted, any previous accidental misinformation corrected, and, in point of accuracy and applicability to their subjects, made pertinent to their present pursuits and the current hour. It will be found, it is trusted, that a recognizable delineation of many of the public characters of the nation,—the "representative men" of their respective classes,—has been faithfully and impartially given.

As to the manner in which Mr. BUNGAY has executed the self-assumed trust, as a noter and critic of "men and measures," the work itself is doubtless the best commentator. With a long and successful experience as a popular advocate of the temperance and other reforms, favored with an enlarged comprehension of the true sphere of individual usefulness, and uniting in his person a well-developed poetic temperament and original imagination,—with a hearty interest in all that elevates and adorns human existence, — it is not surprising that his Sketches, while they are like none other in readable excellence and vivid portraiture, should be permeated with his warm, generous sympathies, and partake conspicuously of his purest heart-aspirations. Thinking thus, his prefacer commits the little work to the favor of the public.

C. W. S.

BOSTON, APRIL, 1852.

CONTENTS.

	Page.
George N. Briggs,	9
John P. Hale,	13
Rufus Choate,	17
Horace Mann,	20
Ralph Waldo Emerson,	24
Horace Greeley,	29
Theodore Parker,	33
John G. Whittier,	38
Neal Dow,	43
Gerritt Smith,	47
Abbott Lawrence,	52
Wendell Phillips,	55
Philip S. White,	60
John Van Buren,	65
William A. White,	69
Edwin H. Chapin,	72
Charles C. Burleigh,	76
William H. Seward,	79
Daniel Webster,	82
Charles Sumner,	86
Moses Grant,	91
John B. Gough,	94

Page.
Lewis Cass, ... 99
Francis Tukey, ... 101
William R. Stacy, ... 103
Elizur Wright, ... 106
John M. Spear, ... 109
John Augustus, ... 112
Father Taylor, ... 114
Elihu Burritt, ... 117
Thurlow Weed Brown, ... 124
Edward Beecher, ... 127
Henry Ward Beecher, ... 131
Massachusetts State Officials, ... 134

Crayon Sketches,

AND

OFF-HAND TAKINGS.

GEORGE N. BRIGGS.

The lives of great men all remind us
We may make our lives sublime,
And, departing, leave behind us
Foot-prints on the sands of time.
LONGFELLOW.

HIS Excellency, GEORGE N. BRIGGS, is an American nobleman in the full-orbed manhood of life. He is robust, of broad build and medium height. His eyes are blue, and his brown hair is tinged with the frost of more than fifty winters. His forehead is wide and high, and indicates more than a mediocrity of intellect, and his countenance is of a serious and thoughtful cast. He dresses plainly, and never wears a collar above his cravat. We attribute this freak of taste to his innate love of liberty. He certainly is unlike the drunkard who was such an ultra republican he would not wear a *crown* in his hat. He belongs to the Baptist church, and is one of its most efficient and influential members. He takes a deep and lively interest in the religious and reformatory movements of the age. In the temperance ranks he has fought many battles and gained many victories. When forgotten as Governor of the glorious old Commonwealth of Massachusetts, he will be gratefully remembered as having been a successful champion of the temperance enterprise.

Gov. Briggs recently manifested a disposition to secure further legislation on the subject of temperance, and he did not handle that question as good old Izaak Walton did the frog he used for a bait, touching it tenderly, as though he would put the hook into his mouth without hurting it. In this way he displeased the publicans and sinners more than he did the friends of the total abstinence cause. He is always right on this question, and deserves great credit for his devotion to the principles of the pledge, and his courageous advocacy of its doctrines. It is difficult for a politician to be a philanthropist, but he is more of the latter than the former. He is not a *bogus* republican, friendly on election days and forgetful at other times. He is not a hypocrite, who spreads palm-leaves in the path of Jesus when he is popular in Jerusalem, and denies him after he is nailed to the cross. He believes men live in the deeds they do, and not in the noise they make; in the thoughts they have, and not in the breaths they draw; in the beatings of a good heart, and not in the throbbings of a gold repeater.

When the Hon. Edward Everett delivered the eulogy on the death of the lamented Adams, every little great man in the city, who had an opportunity to make a display, was bedizened with the tinselry, jewelry and regalia of office; but the Governor, who is a wise man and a good man, wore a plain citizen's dress, marked with a simple badge of mourning. He knows that birth, genius, talent, learning, wealth and personal attractions do not alone make one man better than another. A man may carry a silver-headed cane and wear a wooden head. He may learn the time he squanders from a gold watch, while his heart is as corrupt as a nest of unclean birds. He may have a soft hand at one end of his arm and a softer head at the other. A fool with a fortune is pretty sure to clothe his back more than he cultivates his brains.

Governor Briggs was apprenticed to the hatting business at an early period of his life, and although he afterwards became a lawyer, he never treated working men with disrespect. He loves to grasp the hand hardened by toil, and whether a man's face be bronzed at the plough or bleached in the mill, whether he be clad in ruffles or in rags, he is sure to meet with a warm and welcome and unostentatious reception when introduced to George N. Briggs. He is not so eminent a lawyer as he is a Governor, although he is considered an Aristides in his profession. He is an attractive speaker, and is always ready on all suitable occasions to give free utterance to his manly sentiments. He is more fluent than eloquent, more solid than brilliant, more inclined to labor arguments and relate facts than to round periods and polish sentences. When his voice is not hoarse, and his mind is roused, he will occasionally thrill the heart like a blast from a trumpet.

During his stay in Congress he organized a Congressional Temperance Society, which did a vast amount of good, but, unfortunately, it died out soon after he returned to Massachusetts. In the Sabbath School this distinguished man is "at home." Let the nobles of the land copy his example in this respect, and make themselves useful in their day and generation.

Governor Briggs has, among his political opponents, many personal friends. He doubtless has imperfections, but few public men have less. It is said that he has exercised too much clemency toward convicts whom he has pardoned; if this be a fault it bears toward the side of virtue. Some think his course respecting the Mexican war reprehensible, but this is not the time nor the place to investigate that matter. Some complain that he has not sufficiently imbibed the spirit of anti-slavery, but as we are not all organized, nor educated, nor situated alike, we must make some allowance for differences of opinion. Whatever may be the opinion of some, he will long be remembered as a consistent Christian, and the model Governor of the Old Bay State.

JOHN P. HALE.

JOHN P. HALE is a free-and-easy, fat-and-social man, who can relish a dish of oysters, or a good joke, as well as any member of the Senate. He has the courage of Cromwell, and the fun of Falstaff. He has a strong hand at one end of his arm, and a strong head at the other. When he shakes the former, you feel a heart throbbing in the palm; when he shakes the latter, it is the signal of a storm that will hail (*Hale*) for the space of an hour, and every stone will be the weight of a talent.

Foote may rave and foam, and threaten to hang Hale, his genial and generous fellow Senator, on the tallest tree in Mississippi; but there will be a response so *apropos*, so full of humor, from such a sunshiny countenance, the peppery Mississippian will be ashamed of his impotent imprecations. There is more thunder and lightning in the crack of Hale's joke, than there is punishment in the crack of Foote's pistol. The pungent wit of the former is more destructive than the exploding powder of the latter. The sarcasm and irony of the Northerner is more dreaded than the sulphur and saltpetre of the Southerner. The cool man of "Granite" is more than a match for the choleric representative of "Cotton." The small sword of wit cuts deeper than the bowie-knife of wrath. Foote is a middle-aged gentleman, with a bald head, sear face, shrunken limbs, and restless manners, and so ignitable it is a wonder he had not caught fire and burnt up long ago. Hale is in the prime of life, broad shouldered, broad chested, and stout limbed, and he has such control over his temper he never forgets to be courteous, even to those who permit passion to rule reason, while they sink the glorious dignity of the statesman to the gladiatorial level of the blackguard and the bully. Hale can flog the powdery Senator in debate, and fling him out of the window of the Capitol afterwards, as Commodus threw Cleander out of the Roman palace.

Foote has the most finished education, Hale the most practical sense; Foote has read history and is familiar with the past, Hale has associated with the people and knows the necessities of the present; Foote understands parliamentary usages, Hale observes the rules of the Senate; Foote is nervous, furious and vituperative, Hale is pleasant, manly and earnest; Foote has the rasping severity of Randolph, without his glowing eloquence; the brilliancy of Lee, without his chaste dignity; Hale has the self-reliance of Benton, without, perhaps, his general information. The former is a Cavalier, the latter a Roundhead. One would have fought to the death for King Charles, the other would have united with republican Oliver; one is of the South so extreme as to be tropical, the other of the North so distant as to be frigid. When that great Nebuchadnezzar, the Compromise Bill, with its head of gold, (without brains,) its breast of brass, (without a heart,) its legs of iron, (without stability,) its feet of *Clay*, (without a foothold,) was set up, Mr. Hale refused to bow before it; consequently, he was bound hand and feet, and cast into the heated furnace, but he came out without the smell of fire upon his garments. During the last session of the Senate he was like Daniel (not the Webster) in the lion's den, but he remained uninjured, although there was no angel present to keep the mouths of the animals closed.

Mr. Hale is a man whose telescopic discernment enables him to discover danger at a distance, and when unwise or reckless statesmen plot the ruin of the nation, he sends up a rocket so that its shower of sparks, sheet of fire, and startling report, may attract the attention of the people. When that infamous Compromise Bill was before the Senate, he frequently fired an alarm gun, to warn his constituents and his countrymen. Although he is constitutionally indolent, when his mercury is made to rise to the blood heat of excitement he is a giant, and ordinary men are like grasshoppers in his hands. He has not genius to originate, neither does he display much oratorical skill; but his words drop at the right time and in the right place, as the seed falls from the hands of the sower into the furrow. He puts new wine into old bottles, and bursts them. He is a man for the times, and speaks the language as well as the sentiments of the masses. The man bleached in the factory, and the man bronzed in the foundry, understand him without the aid of an interpreter.

Mr. Hale is sociable and affable in his manners, hearty and pleasant in his address. He has the courage to patronize and defend whatever is designed to promote the welfare of the human race, and the firmness to remain the unfaltering friend to humanity. He speaks fluently and feelingly, and his style and sentiment are both forcible and persuasive. He is a man of foresight and sagacity, and keeps pace with the march of progress. He speaks in behalf of the African race, and pleads for the Abstinence cause.

In personal appearance, Mr. Hale is a large, stout man, somewhat inclined to corpulency; has a full, healthy, rosy face; dark hair, touched with frost; blue eyes, beaming with mirthfulness; an ample chest swelling with a generous heart, and shoulders strong enough to bear the cross of his party.

RUFUS CHOATE.

RUFUS CHOATE is the Brougham of the Western World. He is not so profound a metaphysician or so great a philosopher as the English Lord; but he is equally eloquent, and there is more lightning in his thunder. When he speaks, his black eyes glow with electricity, his hair stands erect as though his head were a galvanic battery, charging each individual hair with the subtile fluid. He is furious as a madman in his gestures, and not unfrequently tears his coat from the collar to the waist, when he becomes intensely excited. He walks from one end of the platform to the other, and swings his arms backwards and forwards as though he intended to take a leap into the middle of the room and land upon the heads of his hearers. If he ever should take a hop-step and jump, in the midst of one of his orations, there would be danger of his tumbling down the throats of some of the gaping multitude, whose mouths are ever open to swallow every syllable he utters. No wonder the people gape and gaze with such astonishment and admiration, for he has such a beautiful gallery of pictures in the chambers of his imagination — such an affluence of language — so retentive a memory — such varied learning — such luminous eloquence and eccentric a manner of delivery. Often, when he finishes a period in his most energetic style, the listener involuntarily looks up to see if the fiery bolt just launched from his lips, has not raised the roof, or at least gone through the ceiling. It is as difficult to report his speeches, as it would be to report the trumpetings of the storm, with the moaning wind, the pattering rain, the vivid lightnings and the crashing of the thunders. He begins like an eagle soaring from his eyrie, and continues his upward flight over the mountain tops, up higher and still higher, and higher still, with the clouds under his feet and a crown of stars about his head; and when he descends, he shines like Moses coming down from the mountain, and like him, he breaks the Commandments when he finds the people worshipping the idol of another party. You may talk about torrents of eloquence — he is the very Niagara of eloquence, with the silver spray, the effulgent bow, and the wasteless waters foaming and flashing through a *narrow channel of rocks.* His speeches are brilliant with unmeasured poetry, and abound in attic wit, biting invective, glowing rhetoric, and logic on fire. "He can hew out a Colossus from a rock, or carve heads on cherry stones." He is not a glancing, dancing stream, fettered with ice half the year; but a magnificent and mighty river, *running South;* and as he sweeps on, he swallows up allusions, quotations, figures, from Hesiod, and Homer, and Virgil, and Voltaire, and Shakspeare, and Milton, and Washington and Webster, still flowing on,

> "Like to the Pontic Sea,
> Whose current and compulsive course
> Never feels retiring ebb, but keeps right on
> To the Propontic and the Hellespont."

To drop the figure and take up the fact, he has intensity of purpose, and often allows his impulsiveness to control his judgment. Every great effort he makes at the Bar or on the rostrum, so excites his nervous system that he cannot sleep sufficiently to satisfy the wants of his physical nature. But he is fond of fame and of money, and seems determined to keep up his reputation and his revenue; consequently his services are available when fair opportunities are afforded for the improvement of either. His speeches sound better than they read. Indeed, it would not be gratifying to the vanity of himself or his numerous friends to pass his extemporaneous speeches through the crucible of criticism. He skips from one topic to another with the agility of a squirrel, a fact unnoticed amid the blaze of his surpassing eloquence, until the storm has passed by and the fever is over, and then we behold the best a reporter can do in the columns of the newspaper.

Mr. Choate is a dark complexioned, thin, cadaverous looking man, with keen black eyes, and a profusion of unkempt hair of a glossy black hue. He is between forty and fifty years of age, and of a nervous billious temperament. He is a conservative Whig of the Webster school, and has made eloquent speeches recently upon the leading political questions of the day. As the Scotch orator once said, I have "neither time nor *space*" to amplify this hastily written sketch, and will conclude with the remark that Mr. Choate is one of the most popular orators of modern times. We have abler lawyers in America, but the Bar has not a more brilliant and successful advocate. We have more experienced statesmen, but few serve their country with more fervid zeal. It is indeed a rich treat to listen to the gorgeous words which drop from his lips like apples of gold in pictures of silver.

HORACE MANN.

THE name and fame of the distinguished subject of this sketch are world-wide. He is known, honored and appreciated as the promoter of education and the defender of the oppressed. The mantle dropped by the lamented Adams sits gracefully upon his shoulders. He is eminent as a writer, a speaker, a scholar and a statesman. His essays and his speeches command the attention and win the admiration of all who read or hear them. He never fails to get the eyes and ears, if not the hearts, of his hearers, whether they be little children in a common school, or larger ones in Congress. He is a prophet who hath honor in his own and other countries. The first time the writer saw him, was at the opening of a primary school in Boston. Several prominent men had spoken to the children present, in unintelligible language; in fact, they spoke to the youths as they were accustomed to speak to adults. By-and-by, a tall, thin, graceful man, with a high forehead and silvery hair, arose in one corner of the room, and in a familiar manner asked the children to let him see their red lips and bright eyes. In a moment a sea of sunny faces was turned toward him. He told them to persevere in the acquisition of knowledge, and asked them if they ever saw a honey-bee go out from its hive on a May morning in pursuit of its sweets. They said they had seen the bee on his tour among the flowers.

"Now," continued the speaker, "when he comes from the leaves he does not bring a whole hive on his back, but he flies home with a little at a time." The children were intensely interested in his stories, comparisons, allusions and admonitions.

The next time I saw this prominent and popular MANN, was at the dedication of a grammar school in Boston. Many of the first citizens were present, and listened with delight to his extemporaneous and appropriate speech. His tongue is like the pen of a ready writer. It costs him little or no effort to round a period handsomely, or polish a sentence until it becomes transparent with beauty, and as for grammatical inaccuracies, even in his impromptu efforts, they are out of the question. Last Winter he delivered the introductory lecture before the Mercantile Library Association. Tremont Temple was packed, from the orchestra to the entrance. Many persons were obliged to leave the crowded doors for want of accommodation. After the usual preliminaries, the orator appeared on the platform and was warmly greeted by the vast audience. He commenced at once by leaping, at a single bound, into the middle of his thesis, and he addressed the young merchants in a strain of surpassing power and eloquence. The last survivor of that large assembly cannot outlive the impression that masterly effort made on every appreciating mind. He spoke forcibly, rapidly, emphatically. Wit, humor, pathos, irony, argument, flowed from his lips as freely as water from an unfailing fountain. Those who carry their souls in the sacs of their stomachs, and those who carry their hearts in their breeches-pockets, were shown up as Marshal Tukey exhibits the light-fingered gentlemen who sometimes visit the City of Notions. He did not spare the wine-bottle nor the tobacco-box, the coffee-pot nor the tea-kettle. He pro-

2

nounced woes against those who will not breathe pure air, and drink cold water, and eat plain food, and sleep on hard beds in ventilated rooms. He has a stout heart and a strong hand, and the whip he holds over the backs of gluttons and imbibers has a silver lash and a golden handle, and although every blow reaches the red, the wounded and the whipped save their lamentations for the secret chamber where they sit upon the stool of repentance.

If it be true that New England is further from perdition and nearer paradise than any other portion of America, it is owing to the superiority of her public schools. Horace Mann has done more than any other person to elevate the educational advantages of New England. His praise is in all the schools. His system of instruction is almost universally adopted. The moral atmosphere of Washington is sure to spoil the principles of some men whom the multitude delight to honor. Not so with Horace Mann. He does not wear a double face. He does not blow hot and cold in the same breath. He does not amend, abridge or alter his speeches to suit the latitude in which he lives. Even the Hercules of the Senate, the mighty Expounder of the Constitution, has felt the weight of his arm and staggered under the force of his blow. Horace Mann not only goes for free soil and free men, but for free air and the free use of cold water. He is liberal-minded, generous-hearted, dignified in his deportment, genteel in his address, and his character is like Cæsar's wife, above suspicion. He is not only admired, but really beloved, by his friends, acquaintances and constituents.

Phrenologically speaking, he has a classical face and forehead. The organ of benevolence is prominently developed, as are the organs of causality, comparison, ideality and sublimity. He is a poet, although he may not have exhibited any symptoms of that sort in rhyme. In his happiest efforts before an audience, he often leads them high up the mountain so that they may see the promised land where the nations shall dwell in the good time coming.

Mr. Mann is a cogent reasoner, a deep thinker, a ready debater, an elegant writer, a splendid speaker. There is a little lisping impediment on his tongue until he becomes excited. Anti-progress men cannot bribe him, nor scare him, nor gag him, nor cope with him at the press or in the forum. He is remarkable for his originality, and his ideas are like pictures painted on glass by those ancients who had the art, now lost, of making the colors penetrate the surface so that the object appeared as vividly on one side as the other. He may be called a "proverbial philosopher," a prose poet, a sayer as well as a doer of good things. Some of the "old liners" in literature and theology, do not approve his liberal sentiments. They have not the courage to assail him openly, but they damn him with faint praise in private circles. He is apt to indulge a taste for alliteration. It is almost the only blemish in his essays and speeches. There is no man in New England so well qualified in every respect to occupy the post of honor and duty rendered vacant by the death of John Quincy Adams, as he.

RALPH WALDO EMERSON.

RALPH WALDO EMERSON is one of the most erratic and capricious men in America. Some of the wiseacres who at first declared him a will-o'-the-wisp, have long since made the discovery that he is a fiery comet of the first magnitude, sweeping through the heavens, and eclipsing the glory of some of the fixed stars in our literary firmament. He is emphatically a democrat of the world, and believes that what Plato thought another man may think, what Paul felt another man may feel, what Shakspeare sang others may know to be true. As for popes, emperors, kings, queens, princes, and presidents, he looks upon them as grown-up children in masquerade, — uncrown them, disrobe them, and bring them on a fair level with their fellow beings, and their superiors may be found among their subjects. In his essay on Self-Reliance, he says: — "Our reading is mendicant and sycophantic in history, our imagination makes fools of us, plays us false. Kingdom and lordship, power and estate, are a gaudier vocabulary than private John or Edward in a small house and common days' works, but the things of life are the same to both. Why all this deference to Alfred and Scanderberg and Gustavus? Suppose they were virtuous, did they wear out virtue?" He has no patience with the chicken-hearted who have to refer to mouldy records and old almanacks to ascertain if they may say their souls are their own. We overlook present good in our insane attempts to pry into the mysteries of the dark past. We put the past in front of our faces, instead of keeping it behind our backs, where it legitimately belongs. Hear him: — "He dare not say I think I am, but quotes some saint or sage. He is ashamed before the blade of grass or blowing rose. These roses under my window make no reference to former roses, or to better ones; they are for what they are; they exist with God to day." "But man postpones or remembers; he does not live in the present, but with reverted eye laments the past, or, heedless of the riches that surround him, stands on tip-toe to foresee the future."

This idealistic philosopher and Titian thinker is not sanguine in his hopes of progress. He has the impression that men say "go," and stand still; that radicals shout "reform," and do not improve themselves; that many Christians go to church for the same reason that the multitude went into the wilderness. If society improves here, it retrogrades there; when the tide of prosperity flows in one place, it ebbs in another. We have maps, charts, books and globes, but neglect to study the beautiful earth and the bright heavens. We go fast, (even by steam,) but what we have gained in speed we have lost in strength; we have acquired a knowledge of science and sacrificed our health; the telegraph is our "errand-boy," and we die for the lack of exercise; we lose our roses in our teens, and grow grey in the morning of life. If we are wiser, we are also older than our fathers were at twice our age. We gape and gaze at every novelty that comes before us. A quack with his nostrums, a priest with his nonsense say to us, "Shut your eyes, open your mouth, and swallow;" and we, like boa-constrictors, swallow

2*

the whole, and then mistake an undigested stomach-full for a heart-full.

Mr. Emerson is a terse, vivid and graphic writer. Sometimes there is a glow of poetry behind a veil of mist in his essays. It is difficult to tell at what he is driving. He is often like the sun in a fog; we know there is light and heat, but the vapor hangs like a thin curtain between us and the luminary, as though the monarch of the skies was trying to hide his spots. He now and then deals in unintelligible inversions, inexplicable mysticisms, and seems to shake up his disjointed and unsorted ideas in ollapodiana style, as though he designed to give us the "clippings, parings and shreds of his thoughts." If Swedenborg be the Shakspeare of theology, Emerson is the Swedenborg of philosophy. Even his incongruous agglomerations are brilliant as they are incomprehensible. Read the following as a specimen of that style:—"The Gothic cathedral is a blossoming in stone, subdued by the insatiable demand of harmony in man. The mountain of granite blooms into an eternal flower, with the lightness and delicate finish as well as the ærial proportions and perspective of vegetable beauty. In like manner all public facts are to be individualized, all private facts are to be generalized. Then at once history becomes fluid and true, and biography deep and sublime."

Mr. Emerson is a poetical as well as a prose writer, but there is more poetry in his prose than in his poems. In Europe he is regarded as *the* essayist of America. During his tour through Great Britain, he met with a cordial reception, and his lectures were numerously attended. He is by some entitled the "Carlyle of America," but he is evidently a better and a greater man than Carlyle. The pupil is wiser than the teacher. The chip is larger than the block.

He has a more opulent intellect, much better taste, and higher and holier aims, than the snarling, cynical philosopher of the Old World.

The only time the writer had an opportunity to hear Mr. Emerson, was at a mass meeting in Worcester. He was invited to speak, and responded with great reluctance, and then made a failure. He stammered, halted, blundered, hesitated, through a five minutes' speech. The people were astonished at his awkwardness. He cannot make an extemporaneous speech. He would not have appeared to such great disadvantage, perhaps, had he not followed directly in the wake of Wendell Phillips. Mr. Emerson is in the prime of life, and is an intellectual-looking man; has dark brown hair, blue eyes, a pale, thoughtful face, not a great development of forehead, and is between forty and fifty years of age. He is a sociable, accessible, republican sort of a man, and a great admirer of nature. Had he been a Persian he would have worshipped the sun. He is celebrated the world over as a lyceum lecturer. He is in independent circumstances. He is a strange compound of contradictions — always right in practice, often right in theory. He is a sun, rising in the East and setting in the West, but occasionally he alarms and astonishes us by rising and shining at midnight.

The literary Lilliputians who have endeavored to pin Emerson to the earth, find that he is in good standing with the gods; of course, their labors, not of love but of jealousy, are lost. He loves his brother man, whether he belongs to the green-jacket tribe or the royal family. He looks upon the flowers as his friends.

"The spendthrift crocus, bursting from the mould,
Naked and shivering with its cup of gold,"

has honey and fragrance for him. The birds are his companions, and he interprets their warblings. He reads the lessons that are stereotyped on the rocks,—in a word, to him the world is a book and the sky its blue cover; deserts and oceans are its fly-leaves, and the busy nations the illustrations of the volume.

HORACE GREELEY.

THE subject of this sketch is the prince of paragraphists — the Napoleon of Essayists. For years he has employed his talents in winding and unwinding the "tangled yarn" of human affairs in Church and State — in Philosophy and Politics — in Art and Literature. He is the great recording secretary of this Continent, employed by the masses to take notes and print them. His business is to "hold the mirror up to Nature, and show the very age and body of the time, its form and pressure." He has the pluck to say as an editor what he feels as a man — when he forgets that he is a politician. It is then that we find truth without concealment, and genuine open-heartedness without wire-working behind the curtain. It is then he

> "—— Pours out all as plain
> As downright Shippen, or as old Montaigne."

Notwithstanding his wayward whims — his eccentric manners — his love of the intangible ideal — his faith in Fourrierism — his responses to spirit rappers — his man-worship when Henry Clay is the human god — he is still the model Editor and the leader of the "press gang;" and the columns of *The Tribune* afford a panoramic view of the American world as it is. Greeley is a pen pugilist, (but never a bully,) and woe betide the unlucky wight that begins the assault. Is he a clergyman? — then duodecimos, octavos and quartos of ecclesiastical history will be hurled at his head, and he cannot dodge them though he makes a coward's castle of the pulpit. Is he a political man? — then he must be right, or he will be flaggellated, if he ventures to measure lances with one who is a walking register and familiar with every important political event that has transpired for the last twenty years. He has more than a usual knowledge of the past. His writings embrace every variety of style, classic beauty, exquisite poetry, graphic description, vapid commonplace, the full sun-blaze of originality, the moon in the mist, and the *ignis fatuus* light of whimsical nonsense. It is but just, however, to say, that he rarely troubles his readers with verbiage or pedantry. He gives us his immediate impressions of things, and his style depends somewhat upon the state of his health and the leisure at his disposal. He does not stop to tack on syllables to make a sentence even, nor measure periods so that they will be as mathematically correct as the vibrations of a pendulum; but he dashes on, heedless of consequences. His widely circulated journal contains good specimens of acute wit, critical reasoning, solid argument, brilliant invective, profound philosophy, beautiful poetry, and moving eloquence, mixed with the opposites of these.

Mr. Greeley is entirely free from heartless bigotry or hypocritical obstinacy. He is benevolent in his disposition, affable and sociable in his manners, often speaks in public, and owing to his fame as a writer, attracts considerable attention; but he is always sure to disappoint his hearers, for he has not sufficient eloquence as an orator, to buoy up the reputation he has won, as a writer. His manner is uncouth, his matter often dry, and his person by no means prepossessing. Here permit me to say, that his careless, slip-shod, slovenly way of dressing his person, has rendered him a man of mark and remark. His white hat and white coat have been immortalized, because they are ever worn and ever lasting. If this Whig prophet had more dignity and more dandyism, he would be less popular with the masses, but a great favorite with uppercrustdom.

Mr. Greeley is a practical printer, and has risen to his present eminence by his untiring industry, his unconquerable perseverance and extraordinary talents. No man in this nation controls public opinion more than he. He is a Grand Marshal in the great army of reformers, not afraid or ashamed to speak — to commit himself, save when his party may suffer by the act. He is a patriot Whig, a philanthropic Whig, a temperance Whig, an anti-slavery Whig, a Whig writer, a Whig speaker, the editor of a Whig paper, and that paper one of the very best in the United States.

No wonder Mr. Greeley knows so well how to meet the wants and wishes of his patrons, *for he has been in the world ever since he was born,* and has been in various situations in life — canal driver* and member of Congress. Mr. Greeley is about forty years of age, of nervous temperament, has a large head — too large for his vital organs — a pale complexion, small eyes sunk under a dumpling forehead, a very scanty supply of very soft, white hair, (not grey,) which will not grow in front, but makes up the deficiency by a patriarchal overgrowth behind.

When the reader beholds a man with an old white hat stuck on the back of the cranium, and leaving the forehead bare, a shirt-collar neckerchiefless and unbuttoned, a vest which looks as though it had been put on with a pitch-fork,

---

* I have been so informed.

a pair of trowsers with one leg stuck in a coarse boot and the other striving in vain to reach the ancle; a coat that seems to have been blown upon his back, and pockets filled with exchange papers — he may be sure he sees Horace Greeley. This gentleman is a dietarian; eats coarse, plain food, drinks nothing but cold water, bathes daily, and sleeps upon a hard bed.

In conclusion, permit me to say, that Mr. Greeley is a man whose virtuous life, abstemious habits, generous deeds and magnificent talents, entitle him to the admiration of his fellow men.

THEODORE PARKER.

> "This, like a public inn, provides a treat
> Where each promiscuous guest sits down to eat;
> And such this mental food as we may call
> Something to all men, and to some men all."
>
> CRABBE.

LET the reader imagine it is Sunday morning. The bells are tolling, and the good church-going people of Boston are wending their way to the various places of worship which are open for religious services. Suppose we spend an hour this forenoon at the Melodeon, and hear the celebrated philanthropist who usually preaches there.

Mr. Parker is seated in an arm-chair on the platform. A Bible and a bunch of flowers are on the desk in front of him, and it is difficult to say before-hand from which of the two he will select his text. He will doubtless glorify the fragrant and beautiful blossoms, and condemn some parts of the inspired volume, before he concludes his address. See him rise slowly and walk gently toward the desk. He now leans upon it, closes his eyes, clasps his hands, and commences prayer, in an inaudible voice. Now the hoarse whisper becomes a low, murmuring sound. Now you hear words and a whole sentence occasionally, and wish you had come earlier so as to have obtained a seat nearer the preacher. Now, by opening your ears and watching his lips attentively, you can hear his prayer; but if God is not present, there is no one there who understands it. It abounds with smart maxims, deep philosophical reflections, pious acknowledgments, earnest invocations, and reverential promises.

He has taken his text and commenced reading his manuscript. His voice is rather husky, and his thick lips seem unwilling to part. He now speaks louder and more distinctly; his lead-like eyes begin to glow with genius, and his bald head seems to shine transparently with thought, while he utters, in choice and classical English, sentiments so new, so strange, so mighty, and so mad with radicalism, incorrigible conservatives are offended. He is a moral Columbus, who discovers whole continents of thought, and is sure to cause mutiny in the ship he sails in, because he ventures so far from the dry land on which most men build their hopes. Indeed, he is regarded as a theological corsair, and most of our great guns have been levelled at him, but he sails on uninjured, amid the roar of their opposition, although he frequently endangers his own immortal life by mistaking a whale's back for a green island. His philosophy and his divinity do not agree, for his philosophy is more divine than his divinity. He has but little faith in any part of Scripture that is not apparently susceptible of interpretations favorable to his peculiar views of religious duty, and does not hesitate to ridicule those passages which come in collision with his "utopian" doctrines. In this way he unintentionally destroys, in the minds of many, all reverence for religion, and obliterates the sense of moral obligation. If his hearers were all learned philosophers, his lectures would be invaluable to them; but they consist of all classes. The wise, who sift the wheat from the chaff, may live under his teaching, but the mass, who swallow every thing he offers, are in danger of suffering all the pangs of spiritual starvation.

He is a true and thorough reformer, and advocates with

great zeal and greater ability the peace reform, the temperance reform, the anti-slavery and anti-hanging reforms. In the course of his sermon he is sure to apply the rod to "Uncle Sam's prize-fighters," the Army and the Navy. The old autocrat Alcohol will be flagellated — the South will receive a blow here — the church will get a whack there — and the gallows will be kicked over yonder. He reminds one of the school-masters of ancient times, but he serves great men as they did little boys. Statesmen, clergymen, aristocrats, are called up and publicly chastised, if they do not say their lessons correctly. A few days ago, Daniel Webster had to hold out his hand and feel the ferule — Gen. Cass is frequently compelled to stand on the dunce-block at the Melodeon — Foote has to wear the cap and bells every time he threatens to hang or shoot his fellow Senators — he pats Benton on the shoulders by way of encouragement, when he speaks for freedom — John P. Hale he thinks is a precocious child of great promise — Ralph Waldo Emerson is so far advanced in knowledge, he would employ him as usher in his school.

Mr. Parker's matter is more fascinating than his manner. Indeed, he is often awkward in his gestures and indistinct in his utterance, but he has the happy faculty of compressing a volume of meaning in a few simple words. He never appears before an audience without giving his hearers at least one drop of fragrance which contains the concentrated essence of a whole garden of roses.

He is the poor man's friend, although he regards poverty as an unmitigated curse,— and would never be like the hypocrites who pass by on the other side when humanity is prostrate, bleeding, and beseeching help. He has an extraordinary share of moral courage, and wages war like a hero, against the kingdom of scoundreldom. He is fond of the company of the gods, and talks about Mars, Jupiter, Neptune, as though they had been his school-mates; is a modern among the ancients, an ancient amongst the moderns; will tell you with perfect coolness, that Paul was not so good a writer as Socrates; that Jesus was a perfect man,—that by-and-by there will be other men as perfect as Jesus; and that the statutes of Moses are not equal to those of Massachusetts. He seems to spurn what he cannot fathom, and condemn what he cannot comprehend. He doubts whether Christ could perform miracles because he cannot perform miracles himself; thinks inspiration is reason magnetized,—the Bible an interesting, but not always reliable history of the Jews,—the popular religion of the times a delusive sham; loves to trace human progress from the barbarous ages to the present time, and then look forward to a golden future. Were he to manifest more reverence for the truths of revelation, and show that he placed as much faith in God as he does in man, he would, with his varied learning and great talents, accomplish an immeasurable amount of good; and many young men who have more faith in a newspaper than they have in the New Testament, would endorse its sentiments and follow the precepts of that heavenly guide.

Mr. Parker is a chaste and elegant writer, his works are widely circulated and read by scholars on both continents. Although he is denounced as an infidel by his opponents, he certainly behaves like a Christian in his private intercourse with his fellow men. He thinks there is nothing in the world so sacred as man, which accounts for the fact that he hates flogging in the Navy, and is opposed to hanging, and oppression, and intemperance, and the butchery of the battle-field.

He is upwards of forty years of age, rather under the

medium stature, head large and bald, and his face dull, until he becomes animated before an audience; is quite popular as a lyceum lecturer, and is in great demand during the lecturing season.

The subject of this sketch, though wrong in theory, is right in practice, and has courage enough to seize the social and public evils by the throat. We, as a community, are deeply indebted to him for his efforts to improve the condition of the unfortunate. He "goes" for baths, ventilators, hard beds, coarse food, cold water, and cheerfulness, and "goes" against tobabco, hot slops, quack medicines, thin shoes, and tight lacing; hates bigotry, gluttony, drunkenness, poverty, war, and slavery, and loves purity, fidelity, liberty, equality, fraternity. He is one of the most learned and gifted men in America, and is a better Christian than some of his bigoted detractors, who say he is like Noah's carpenters, who built a ship for other folks to sail in, and yet were drowned themselves.

JOHN GREENLEAF WHITTIER.

"THERE," said our driver, "is the birth-place of John G. Whittier," when he pointed to a plain farm-house on the edge of the town of Haverhill, situated a short walk from the roadside,—or, as the poet himself describes the old homestead,—"Our farm house was situated in a lonely valley, half surrounded with woods, with no neighbors in sight."

Soon after my arrival at the busy and beautiful village of Amesbury, where the great poet of humanity now lives, I ascertained his whereabouts, and gave him a letter of introduction, written by our mutual friend, W. A. W——, an untiring co-laborer in the work-field of reform. I found him at home, in his modest little Quaker cottage, where his friends and visitors are sure to meet with a kind reception. On the adjoining lot is another nest in the bushes, where a family of singers give vocal utterance to the poetry Whittier writes. Mr. W. responded to the rap at the door, and invited me to take a chair in a plain, neat room, which commands a view of a large and beautiful garden, where he spends a share of his leisure time, when his health will permit him to work there. He gave me an introduction to his excellent mother, and, after a little chat on the common topics of conversation, politely invited me to remain and take tea with him.

I knew quite well that I was in the presence of one of the purest-minded and most gifted men in America; a man whose name and fame are world-wide, and "as familiar as household words;" a man whose mighty thoughts are winged with words of fire; but he was so unassuming, so accessible, so frank, and so well "posted up" on all matters of news, that, whatever subject is broached, one feels at home in the presence of a *friend*, while conversing with him. This eminent poet of the slave is about forty years of age. His temperament is nervous-bilious; is tall, slender, and straight as an Indian; has a superb head; his brow looks like a white cloud, under his raven hair; eyes large, black as sloes, and glowing with expression. He belongs to the society of Friends, and in matters of dress and address, he is a Quaker of "the strictest sort." Should a stranger meet him in the street, with his collarless coat and broad-brimmed hat, he would not discover anything remarkable in his appearance, certainly would not dream that he had seen the Elliott of America. But, let him uncover that head, and see those star-like eyes flashing under such a magnificent forehead, and he would know, at a glance, that a great heart, a great soul, and a great intellect, must light up such a radiant frontispiece. His fellow townsmen are proud of his fame, and well they may be, for Amesbury will be known all over the world, to the end of time, as the residence of John G. Whittier, "the poet of the poor."

Wherever he discovers the talisman of intellect he recognizes a brother; "though his skin and bones were of the color of night, they are transparent, and the everlasting stars shine through them with attractive beams." He knows that complexion is not a crime, crisped hair is not a sin, thick lips are not a transgression, and he has bared his arms to avert the blow that would plough the quivering flesh of the toil-worn slave. He has heard the wail of the distracted mother, who, like Rachel, refuses to be comforted because her child has been torn from her bosom and sold into hopeless servitude, where her eye cannot pity its sorrows, where her hand cannot alleviate its distress; and he has denounced such fiendish cruelty with an eloquence and pathos approximating to inspiration. He has seen hollow-hearted statesmen tear the stripes from our flag and put them on the backs of our countrymen, and he has spiced sheets that will preserve such mummies in the amber and pitch of infamy forever. He has seen the fugitive flying from the house of bondage, with hunters and blood-hounds on his track in hot pursuit, and he has shouted, "God speed the slave!" until lungless echo has repeated the cry on every hill-top of the free North. He has seen where the red-hot branding-iron has been pressed on the shrinking flesh of a freeman's hand, until the sizzling blood spouted from the wound, and the angel of his muse touched his lips with a burning coal from the altar of God, whilst he immortalized the patient hero, and annihilated everything but the damnable infamy of the heartless, soulless persecutors.

Mr. Whittier is a sincere lover of truth and right, and his language is, "In vain and long, enduring wrong, the weak may strive against the strong, but the day shall yet appear, when the might with the right and the truth shall be, and come what there may to stand in the way, that day the world shall see." (Pardon my drawing the lines into prose. I quote from memory, and fear I might do still greater injustice to the author by measuring the sentiment off into verse.) Such men as he, are excluded from the South, but slaveholders can no more keep out his sentiments than the fool could keep the wind out of the barn-yard by closing the gate. Judging by the emotions excited by his writings, we are led to the conclusion that he usually writes with tears in his eyes, but a certain magazine publisher, whose likeness accompanied one of the numbers of his magazine, can testify that his satire punishes like the sting of a scorpion. Read the following lines: —

"A moony breadth of virgin face,
By thought unviolated,
A patient mouth to take from scorn
The hook with bank-notes baited,—
Its self-complacent sleekness shows
How thrift goes with the fawner,
An unctuous unconcern for all,
Which nice folks call dishonor."

An eminent statesman will find it difficult to outlive the following lines: —

"So fallen, so lost! the light withdrawn
Which once he wore!
The glory from his grey hairs gone
Forever more.

Let not the land once proud of him
Insult him now,
Nor brand with deeper shame his dim,
Dishonored brow.

But let its humbled sons instead,
From sea to lake,
A long lament as for the dead,
In sadness make.

Then pay the reverence of old days
To his dead fame;
Walk backward with averted gaze,
And hide the shame."

Whittier's poetry is eloquence measured with a golden reed, logic on fire, pathos crying in the notes of the nightingale, philosophy playing on the harp, humor laughing in numbers, wit rained down from heaven in a shower of stars. His writings are not free from imperfections of style and sentiment; but men seldom notice pebbles while they look at the lights in the cerulean arch above. He is the author of several volumes of prose, which are widely circulated. His verses are full of philosophy, beauty, and sublimity. He sympathizes with the unfortunate, and chastises the oppressor with a whip of adders. In some of his patriotic appeals he reminds us of the old prophets. Had Isaiah lived in these times, he might have written the following lines without impairing his reputation: —

"Now, by our fathers' ashes! where's the spirit
Of the true-hearted and the unshackled gone?
Sons of the old freemen, do we but inherit
Their *names* alone?

Is the old Pilgrim spirit quenched within us?
Stoops the proud manhood of our souls so low
That mammon's lure or party's wile can win us
To silence now?

No! When our land to ruin's brink is verging,
In God's name let us speak while there is time!
Now, when the padlocks for our lips are forging,
SILENCE IS CRIME!"

Some of his best poems have been published in beautiful style in Boston lately, but the work is so expensive the masses are not able to buy it. His writings do not need such costly embellishments to be appreciated, any more than the sun needs a stained window through which to shine. The lark and the nightingale need not the costume of the peacock to ensure admiration. Mr. Whittier is one of the editors of the *National Era*, and I may say, in whisper, to the ladies, he is a — bachelor.

NEAL DOW.

The man who has the talent to frame and the courage to execute the Maine Law, deserves to be honored and remembered by every patriot and philanthropist in our broad free land. Neal Dow is the Kossuth of the temperance revolution, and his name is already registered in the book of fame, "among the few, the immortal names not born to die." Poets sing his praise, painters put his shadow on their canvass — historians record his deeds, and multitudes of appreciating mothers will call their children by his name.

We wrote pledges, made speeches, obtained signatures, formed societies, and framed laws, to suppress intemperance; we tried moral, magnetic, Bible, and ballot-box suasion; we plead, and prayed, and promised, and did incalculable good, but failed to accomplish the entire extinction of the rum traffic, the object so devoutly desired. We were brought to a moral Panama, with a gulf of billows rolling between us, and a golden California beyond, without bridge or boat to carry us safely over to the land of promise, when Neal Dow, who understood every rope in the ship, took the helm and piloted our storm-beaten vessel into the harbor of safety.

Yes, a private citizen of Maine, possessing the stern will and Puritan zeal "of the earlier and better day," arose in the dignity of conscious strength, and with the sweep of his strong arm wiped away the stain of black intemperance from the State. Without the aid of the Army or the Navy, he routed the most formidable and dangerous enemy that could assail the Commonwealth.

Lean and pallid avarice, haggard appetite, stupid ignorance, bloated bigotry, devilish demagogueism, stood in his way, clad to the teeth in armor, but he feared them no more than Bunyan's Christian feared the beasts he met on his way to the Celestial city. He extinguished the fires of the only distillery in the State, and wrote *tekel* on the walls of every wine palace in Maine. Who is this modern Moses who smote the Red Sea with the rod of the law, so that the people can travel dry-shod? He is a man who has a head to think, a heart to feel, a tongue to explain, and a hand to execute; is respectably educated, not learned, comfortably independent, not a millionaire; speaks conversationally, not eloquently; is a plain, practical man, with a strong mind and an iron will. Had he lived in the days of Cromwell, he would have been a leader in the battered band that fought side by side with the "Usurper." He speaks as one having authority, and looks like one born to command. He is in the meridian of life — about five feet seven inches in height, and well proportioned; has dark hair, a square forehead, which does not at first glance indicate more than a mediocrity of mind; eye-brows are rather ponderous, cheek bones somewhat prominent, complexion dark. The peculiar form of the mouth and chin pronounce him a man of obstinate firmness. There is a sort of *come on, I am ready for you,* look about his face, which affords unmistakeable evidence that he will not *countenance* the liquor trade. He looks as though he could chase a thousand rum sellers, and with the aid of the Maine Law, put ten thousand to flight.

Neal Dow is the son of a Quaker, and surely he fights valiantly for one who has been trained to observe the principles of peace. He does not claim religious relationship with any sect, but is a firm believer in the truths of Divine Revelation, and observes devotional duties in his family. For many years he has been identified with the temperance movement in Maine, (his native State,) where he has labored and lectured gratuitously, for the welfare of his fellow citizens. Frequently has he appeared before the Legislature with petitions praying for laws so stringent as to prohibit the liquor trade, and finally he succeeded in cutting out some work for his country.

He is a tanner by trade, and although he has (I may be misinformed) retired from business, he has left the hides of many rumsellers on the fence. Wonder if they would not make good shoes, since they are water proof! There is not a lawyer in the land who could have drafted a better bill than that which has so effectually excommunicated intemperance from the glorious State which is the nearest to the golden gates of sunrise. The Law declares that intoxicating drinks shall not be made and sold, to be used as a beverage, in Maine — that an agent shall be appointed in each city or town to sell spirits for mechanical and medicinal purposes only — that common sellers shall be heavily fined and imprisoned for persisting in violating the law — that no lawless rum seller shall be allowed to sit as a juror on a rum suit — that liquors may be searched for, seized and destroyed — that in case of appeal, bonds must be given that the case will be prosecuted, and if the judgment goes against the defendant, he must pay double the fine and suffer double the imprisonment, &c., &c. Read the law, it is a good one. It has not been pared down by abridgment, or patched up with amendments. It is the people's law, and not the law of politicians. It is a terror to those who do ill, and a praise to those who do well. It is a fire annihilator, and works well out doors or in, and the effect is the same whether the building be a small one or a large one. Success to the MAIN LAW, which is the *Law of Maine*.

GERRIT SMITH.

On my return from the West, I called to see that generous philanthropist, eminent orator, and impracticable radical, Gerrit Smith. I found him in his office, pen in hand, at his writing-desk. When he read my note of introduction, he remarked that he was familiar with my name, and supposed I was a much older man. He politely invited me to avail myself of his hospitality. I did so, and had an opportunity of seeing him *at home*.

Mr. Smith lives in a small white house, about two miles distant from the village of Peterboro'. It is plainly and sparingly furnished. There are no luxurious sofas upon which to lounge, no costly carpets upon which to tread, no costly mirrors at which to gaze. Everything about his residence partakes of the useful rather than the ornamental. I found him an accessible, sociable, pleasant man, thoroughly familiar with the history of the reformers and the reformatory movements of the present day.

It is well known that this distinguished man stands at the head of the most radical class of reformers. Indeed he stands out so far in front of his age that slow-moving conservatives cannot appreciate the man nor his motives. He denounces rum-patronising and pro-slavery churches; consequently all the anathema maranathas of unsympathizing and unsanctified professors of religion are hurled at his head, and he is condemned as an infidel, whereas he evidently is an humble and devoted follower of Christ. "By their fruits ye shall know them." He asks a blessing at his table. Night and morning he lays the sacrifice of a broken and contrite heart on the altar of family devotion. Every day he carefully studies the Scriptures; and manifests his love to God whom he has not seen, by his love toward his brother-man whom he has seen.

Few men have done more than Mr. Smith to assist the poor, to clothe the naked, to feed the hungry, reform the drunkard and liberate the bondman. The hotels owned by him in different towns and cities in this country, are invariably rented for half the sum liquor-landlords would pay for the same premises. In this way, he has cheerfully sacrificed thousands of dollars to promote the temperance cause. I have not mentioned his munificent donations and eloquent lectures directed to the same object. This model man gave three thousand farms to the same number of black persons, and now he offers a thousand farms and ten thousand dollars to a thousand white persons in the State of New York. Mr. Smith's father was in partnership with John Jacob Astor, at one period of his life. When he died, he bequeathed to the subject of this sketch three quarters of a million acres of land.

In point of intellect, Mr. Smith ranks with such men as Clay and Benton. His mind is comprehensive and well cultivated. His temperament volcanic, but usually controlled by an acute judgment. As an orator he has but few superiors. His manner is deliberate and dignified—his matter choice and classical—his personal appearance noble and attractive. He is about six feet tall, and of perfect proportions; forehead high and broad; eyes large, dark, and expressive; hair brown, and cropped close to his head. At the time I saw him he wore a suit of bottle-green, and his broad shirt-color lay down like a large snow-flake over a black neckerchief. He never decorates his person with the tinselry and jewelry of fashion. He eats plain food, sleeps on a hard bed, bathes every day, drinks nothing but *cold water*, walks from four to ten miles a day, writes from fifty to two hundred letters per week, furnishes long and labored communications for the press, speaks frequently at public meetings.

It is not often we find a man with such immense wealth at his command, sympathizing as he does with his less fortunate fellow men. He believes that man is as much entitled to the earth as he is to air and water, and desires to see every man own a house and lot; is opposed to tariffs, and advocates with great zeal and eloquence the doctrine of free trade; believes there is "a good time coming" when the clarion of war shall cease, and the olive-trees shall grow above mouldering bones on battle-fields; when degrading poverty shall hide its diminished head, and smiling competence shall find all men sitting under their own vines and fig-trees, none daring to molest or make them afraid; when slavery shall no longer bind on heavy burdens; when intemperance shall be among the things that were, and abstinence principles shall universally prevail. With such views, it may not be expected that he always travels on a smooth road and sleeps on a bed of roses. He stirs up the old hornet-nests of hunkerism and awakens the slumbering dog-kennels of conservatism, so that he frequently hears the buzzing of insects and the baying of hounds.

Unimprovable, incorrigible conservatives, who cling to

4*

grey old customs and straight roads, who hate an uneven pathway although it may be the safest and the nearest, remind one of the rats of Norway, that travel in millions from the hills toward the the ocean.* They turn neither to the right nor the left, but gnaw their way through barns and corn-fields, swimming or sailing over rivers, climbing walls and mountains, sweeping through crowded thoroughfares, tumbling from the roofs of houses. On, on, rolls the wave of rats, leaving behind nothing but dead carcases and a foul atmosphere. Man is a progressive animal, and the more conservative he is, the nearer he approximates to the unintellectual brute, and the further he recedes from established laws. God made man upright, and furnished him with a capital of bones and brains with which to commence life. Experience, observation and reflection taught him that Winter would freeze him, Summer scorch him, fire burn him, water drown him, the wild beast devour him, and the avalanche crush him. He robed himself in garments to protect him from the cold of the North and the heat of the South. He built a house for his comfort and protection. He domesticated the dog, the cow and the horse, for his own accommodation. He dried venison and fish, sowed seed and reaped harvests, and continued his progressive movements until the rude hut became a stately palace, the bark canoe a mighty ship with sails and masts, the clumsy cart a city on wheels drawn by steam-steeds over iron roads. Steam is our horse, lightning our herald, water our servant, and the sun our portrait-painter.

Reform tunnels our mountains, levels the hills, lifts up the valleys, and flings its floating bridges of steel and steam and flame and smoke over the oceans. Our railroads are iron

---

* Carlyle.

bands binding us in the bonds of universal brotherhood. Our electric wires are so many nerves of sensation, reaching from the body politic to the brains of society.

Mr. Smith is one of the few who keeps pace with the march of improvement, and he heartily employs his purse, pen and tongue in behalf of free trade, free soil, free types, free lips, and free men. He believes the Constitution is an "anti-slavery document;" so do the free-soil abolitionists, yet is not a "free-soiler." He believes the church is pro-slavery, and on that question agrees with the Garrisonians, but he does not belong to that party. He is at the head of the "Liberty party," and his creed embraces every degree of reform, from the use of cold water as a beverage and in the bath, to the emancipation of three millions of men.

ABBOTT LAWRENCE.

THE first time the writer saw ABBOTT LAWRENCE, the great cotton-lord, was in Brattle Square church. He was standing in the broad aisle, conversing with a negro, who is a brother member of the same religious society to which the subject of this sketch belongs. While the beauty and fashion, the wealth and wisdom, the virtue and piety of that church were pressing homewards, the distinguished man who is now at the Court of St. James, was holding a brief *tête-à-tête* with his black brother, and I had a fine opportunity to take his portrait.

Mr. Lawrence is a tall, portly, noble and dignified-looking man, about sixty years of age. His head is bald, and shines as though it came fresh from the hands of a skilful varnisher and polisher; and it is quite evident that the shining qualities of the head are not confined to the exterior of the skull, but seem rather to result from something brilliant within. He has a calm, pleasant face, indicating, to the minutest line, that he is not afraid to see the sheriff or the clamorous creditor. He wore, on this occasion, a thin cravat, light vest, and a dress coat (I think) of olive green.

I saw him again at a "mass meeting" in Faneuil Hall, the very time when he said his breeches-pocket contained the *evidence* that Gen. Taylor was a Whig! The old

"Cradle of Liberty" was packed with people. It was no easy task for those who came late to gain admittance, but, being accustomed to crowds, and determined to see and hear the speakers, I pushed my way through to the front gallery, where I obtained a seat and a view of the platform. Our subject was in the chair, and in more senses than one he filled it well. He was surrounded by men well known to fame. Some of them were acquainted with him when he was a poor, awkward boy, employed as a clerk in a store in the city of Boston. One of them told the writer that when Mr. Lawrence left his native town of Groton, he came to the capital of Massachusetts with a pair of buckskin gloves on his hands. It was during the Summer season, and some of the city gents. laughed at the verdancy of the country lad. That he afterwards *pulled off* his gloves, the "cities of spindles" he has erected bear the most unequivocal testimony.

At the proper time he arose and made a speech. It contained humor, pathos, and logic enough to be *interesting*. He is more of a business than a literary man; a better financier than statesman, and would never have been more than a moderate statesman if he had not been a first-rate financier. He is indebted to his brains for his money, and to his money for his honors. He went through the mill first, then graduated at the counting-house, and recently journeyed to London as minister-plenipotentiary.

Mr. Lawrence is a magnificent man. He does everything by wholesale and nothing in the retail line. Not satisfied with the murmuring of a single mill, he must make every idle stream turn a crank for him. Look at Lowell and Lawrence, the cities erected by his enterprise! He would not be Mayor of Boston, but he would like to be President of the United States; — is liberal to the poor, though he will not allow his funds to filter through his own hands to the needy. He prefers giving a large sum when he gives anything, but it must be distributed by those who are willing to come in contact with the sorrowing and distressed.

Mr. Lawrence is a practical business man, of pleasing manners and polite address. Although he has devoted a large portion of his life to business, he is familiar with the modern history of nations, and knows enough respecting the etiquette of courts and the usages of diplomacy to fill the station he occupies with credit to himself and honor to his country.

WENDELL PHILLIPS.

WENDELL PHILLIPS is the Patrick Henry of New-England. If he has less natural eloquence, less thrilling pathos, than the orator of the Revolution, he has more polish and as much power of origination. He is a ripe scholar, a lawyer of no ordinary calibre, a magazine writer of considerable note, and a reformer of the most radical school. He is the pet speaker of the East. He has great power of perception, sincere sympathy for the oppressed, and wonderful command over the stores of varied knowledge treasured up in his retentive memory. He has the "gifts that universities cannot bestow," the current coin that cannot be counterfeited, "the prophet's vision," the poet's fancy, the light of genius. He is at home on the mountain-top, and when he soars skyward he is not lost among the clouds; has all the sagacity of the man of business united with the enthusiasm of the utopian, and seems to be equally related to Maia the eloquent, and Jupiter the thunderer. He admires the eternal, the infinite, the heaven-like, the God-approximating in the nature of man, whatever may be the color of the envelope that contains these attributes.

Mr. Phillips' speeches have in them the breath of life — hence they live long to swell the bosom and make the heart throb. "He does not go to the lamp of the old schools to light his torch, but dips it into the sun, which accounts for its gorgeous effulgence." He is something of a metaphysician, but is too much absorbed in the work of revolutionizing public sentiment to devote his attention to subtle research and profound analysis. He makes but little preparation, and always speaks extemporaneously; consequently some of his addresses are like a beautiful damsel in *dishabille;* then his quotations are ringlets rolled up in papers, and the main part of the lecture like a loose gown which now and then reveals a neck of pearl and a voluptuous bust of snowy whiteness and beautiful proportions. He is often brilliant, never tedious. Sometimes his scholarship is seen conspicuously, but it is never pompously displayed.

It is a rich treat to hear Wendell Phillips speak to a large and appreciative audience. Let the reader fancy he is at a mass meeting in some forest temple. The sun shines as though delighted with the gathering; the shy birds perch in silence on the neighboring trees, as though they were astonished at the proceedings; a song makes the welkin ring. The chairman announces the name of a favorite speaker. A genteel man steps gracefully upon the platform. He is neatly, not foppishly, dressed. A pleasant smile illuminates his noble face. He leaps, at a single bound, into the middle of the subject. He reasons, and his logic is on fire; he describes, and the subject is daguerreotyped on the retina of memory; he quotes from some classic author, and the excerpt is like an apple of gold in a picture of silver; he tells a story, and the impression it gives is indelible; he makes an appeal, and tears flow freely; he declaims, and the people are intensely excited; he soars, and his lips are touched with a live coal from the altar of inspiration. Mr. Phillips believes in a "higher law," so he appeals to the sense of the everlasting in man. "He plays the Titanic game of rocks, and not a game of tennis-balls," and yet he "floods the heart with singular and thrilling pleasure." "He is the primed mouth-piece of an eloquent discharge, who presents, applies the linstock, and fires off;" and the conservatives who stand with their fingers in their ears, are startled by the report. Is there a mob? his words are like oil on the troubled billows of the chafed sea; he rebukes the winds of strife and the waves of faction, and there is a great calm. The serene face of his bosom-friend, the leader of the league, is radiant with smiles; the severe front of a turncoat or a tyrant present begins to relax; the doughface is ashamed of himself, and determines that hereafter he will be "a doer and not dough;" the stiff-limbed finds a hinge in his joints, and his supple knees bow in homage to the speaker.

But I must find some fault, or I shall be deemed a flatterer. Let me see — what shall I say? "Oh, he is an impracticable radical; he goes for the dissolution of the Union, the dismemberment of the church, the destruction of the political parties." In this he is partly right and partly wrong. The Christian should do for Christ's sake what the worldling does for the sake of humanity, then there will be no necessity for such a reproof. The body politic should sever the leprous limb of slavery, and then America would not limp so as to become a laughing-stock and a by-word to the nations of the earth. The political parties at the North are leavened with anti-slavery doctrines, and it is hoped they will soon rise to the level of that benevolence which will render such rebukes unnecessary. I declare it is difficult for me to find any fault in him. Reader, you may be Herod, but I cannot be Pilate, and consent to his crucifixion. I must confess that I love the man, although I cannot endorse all his creed. It is a pity that he limits his usefulness by his fierce warfare against men and measures that are too long or too short for his iron bedstead.

Mr. Phillips is a man of fortune, and one of the distinguished few who contributes to support the enterprise in which he feels an interest as much as he expends in sustaining himself and family. Physically he is a noble specimen of a man. His head is sparingly covered with reddish hair, —

> "The golden treasure nature showers down
> On those foredoomed to wear Fame's golden crown."

A phrenologist would pronounce his head worth more than the South would be willing or able to give for it. He has large ideality and sublimity, hence he soars; large comparison and causality, so he reasons by analogy; large hope and benevolence, and the genial sunshine of good-nature irradiates his countenance; large firmness and adhesiveness, and he abides by his friends through evil and through good report. His face is pleasant, and indicates exquisite taste, pure generosity, and Roman firmness. He is now in the full vigor of manhood, and ever ready at a moment's warning to battle for what he deems the right. Woe be unto the man who enters the arena with him, for he wields a two-edged sword of Damascus steel. Many strong men have been slain by him; yea, many mighty men have fallen before him. Had he united with either of the great political parties, he would have been chosen as a champion, for he is brilliant as Choate, without his bedlamitish idiosyncrasies; clear as Clay, without his accommodating, compromising disposition; learned as Winthrop, without his bookishness and drawing-room mannerism; genial as Cass, without his dulness; fiery as Benton, without his unapproachable self-sufficiency. He would entertain a promiscuous audience better than either of the above-named men. He is not so logical as Webster; not so luminous as the ever-consistent Calhoun; not so learned as the second Adams; not so thrilling as Kentucky's favorite; and yet he is a more instructive and a more interesting speaker than either of those distinguished men ever were, even in their palmiest days.

Wendell Phillips is universally esteemed and beloved. Even those who hate his creed, and dread his power, admire his disinterested kindness and irresistible eloquence.

PHILIP S. WHITE.

Everybody said, "Let us go to the great meeting at Tremont Temple, this evening, and hear Philip S. White, the distinguished champion of the temperance reform." At the appointed hour, that magnificent forum was filled with the wealth, beauty, talent, and moral worth of Boston. The immense building was brilliantly illuminated, as though the sun had risen behind the orchestra and concentrated its rays within the walls of the Temple. On the platform were some of the *élite* and *literati* of society,—authors, orators, and philanthropists. After the usual preliminaries, at the commencement of the exercises, skilful fingers touched the magic keys of the mammoth organ, and we were pleasantly entertained with sweet strains of delightful melody. Sometimes it seemed as if a choir of soft-voiced maidens was enclosed behind those golden columns, singing such rich, lute-like airs that angels, on their mission of mercy, might have mistaken that place for the gate of heaven. Then the heavy bass would roll like a wave of thunder through the large hall, startling the charmed hearers to a sense of the fact that they were still under the clouds.

As the music subsided, a tall, portly man, on the mellow side of fifty, arose to address the audience. "Is that the man who stood at the head of the Order of the Sons of

Temperance?" is the general inquiry. "It is," was the response. The "observed of all observers," on this occasion, is a person of good mould, somewhat bald, but makes up that deficiency by a luxurious growth of whiskers, which become his face as feathers do an eagle. He has a large, aquiline, Bardolphian nose, dark eyes, and a wide mouth, indicative of eloquence and good nature. He commences in a conversational pitch of voice; face dull and passionless as marble; has spoken ten minutes without *saying any thing*, and the sanguine expectations of the people are sadly disappointed. The hearers bow their heads like bulrushes, and some would leave the meeting but that they *hope* for better things. He is not quite so prosy now as he was fifteen minutes ago. His voice is deeper and clearer, his utterance more rapid and distinct, and his face shines as though it had been freshly oiled. There is a resurrection now among the bowed heads; he has just made a thrilling appeal, which moved the audience like a shock from an electric battery. Now he relates a tale of pity, which is drawing tears from eyes "unused to weep." Now he surprises his attentive hearers with an unanticipated stroke of humor, which makes them laugh until they shake the tear-drops from their cheeks. All are glad they came now, for the orator is in his happiest mood, his blood is up, and his tongue as free as the pen of a ready writer. He throws light on the question by the corruscations of his attic wit; drives home a truth by solid argument, and clinches it by a quotation from Scripture; convulses the auditory by using a ludicrous comparison; convinces them by presenting sober-faced statistics; entertains them by relating an appropriate anecdote, and fires their indignation against the traffic, while the rum-dealers present shake in their shoes. He warns the drinkers with a voice which arouses them like a clap of thunder through a speaking-trumpet. In a word, his sparkling satire, keen wit, eloquent declamation, happy comparisons, classical allusions, rib-cracking fun, and heart-melting pathos, render him one of the most efficient public speakers in America.

Mr. White can labor a syllogism, or tell a story, with the same ease that Talleyrand could turn a coffee-mill or a kingdom. He goes for moral, legal, bible, pocket, and ballot-box suasion. His inimitable histrionic powers enable him to tell a story admirably. He has almost omnipotent power in swaying the minds and hearts of his hearers, when he is fairly engaged and has a sea of crystal faces before him. He speaks without notes, and is so careless, withal, that he preserves no minutes of his speeches; consequently, when he responds to a second invitation to visit a place, he is apt to repeat the same stories, although he has an inexhaustible supply of unused material always on hand. He has studied human nature so thoroughly he knows how to reach the hearts of the masses. If the people will but listen to his lectures, they will open their mouths so earnestly he could almost reach their hearts by the way of the œsophagus. Mr. White is personally known on the green mountains of Vermont, on the granite hills of New Hampshire, in the pleasant valley of the Connecticut, on the banks of the Mississippi; has hosts of friends at the sunny South, at the stormy North, and the far-off West. Years ago he made the tour of Europe. At that time he was fond of luxurious living and unweaned from the wine-cup; he was a good judge of Otard and Madeira, and can speak from personal experience on matters pertaining to fashionable drinking.

Mr. White is a good specimen of a Kentucky gentleman — gallant, generous and urbane. Indeed, he can accommodate himself to any company, and would be a welcome guest at the table of a duke, or feel perfectly at home in the cottage of a peasant. He must have been a studious man in his day, but he has bravely overcome that habit now; for he would rather hold a man by the button all day, entertaining him by telling stories, than to read a page or write a "stick-full" of matter for a newspaper. When he has a report to make, he will throw the burden, if he can possibly do so, on shoulders not so able to bear it as his own, and he will put off the unwelcome task to the last hour, then dash off an impromptu report, and beauty will break out of statistics and facts, like flowers on the rod of Aaron. Sometimes he visits Subordinate Divisions of his favorite Order, as well as Sections of the juvenile Cadets, to fire the zeal, strengthen the faith, and encourage the hopes of the "Sons" and their sons. I once heard him address one of the latter societies on the evils arising from the use of tobacco, but, unfortunately, he had that evening quite a *gathering* in his own mouth, which somewhat choked his utterance. The not altogether *unusual* swelling somewhat disappeared before the meeting adjourned, and it is hoped that by this time he has got entirely rid of the swelling.

Mr. White is good company, a good story-teller, and a terror to all hypochondriacism and dyspepsia. Blessed are they who hear his voice and see his face, for they shall laugh and grow fat. I am no stickler for empty dignity, but remain under the impression that Mr. W. is not so dignified at the fireside as he is in the forum. There are vulgar persons who call him the *Hon.* Philip S. White when they speak of his public efforts, and yet abbreviate the title to *Phil.* in their personal intercourse with him. He is no favorite with those who will not "give up a 'pint' of doctrine nor a pint of rum," for as the bottle-imp of Asmodeus unroofed the houses of Madrid, for the gratification of Le

Sage's servant, so he uncovers the hearts of those whose bigotry or appetite or interest oppose the temperance reformation. Mr. White is by profession a lawyer, and, if I am correctly informed, was at one period of his life Attorney General of one of the Western Territories. He is proud of his lineage, and is not backward in speaking about his former position in society, which is in bad taste, since he is now in a loftier position than any Baronet of England.

The fraternity, I think, manifested forecast worthy of their trust when they selected him to be their leader, for his abundant self-sacrificing and faithful labors in this country and in the neighboring Provinces, have accomplished incalculable good to the cause in general, and won unfading laurels for him in particular. He is the author of a work entitled the "War of Four Thousand Years," and a tract entitled "Vindication of the Order." It is a pity that he did not give a more Christian name to the first, and a matter of regret that he went into partnership with others in writing either. His admirers would like to see a book from his own pen and know that he wrote it. His idea of a national newspaper organ, to be managed by some master-mind of the National Division, does not meet with general approval, because it would be unwise to put such power into the hands of one man; because it would narrow the circulation of the local papers to the starving point; because one sheet would not suit every meridian; because the temperance press now in operation is not properly sustained; because there is a much editorial tact and talent connected with the local press as can be found in the National Division; because monopolies are monsters not favorable to the growth of Love, Purity or Fidelity, the characteristics of our Order.

JOHN VAN BUREN.

PRINCE JOHN is the Duke of York, the distinguished son of King Martin the First; — is the Jupiter Tonans of his party, the Jove of jolly fellows, a royal roystering republican, a genius and a good fellow, admired and adored by the masses. He can accommodate himself to the society of the voters in the "Sixth Ward," or the company of peers with laced gauntlets, knights in golden mantles, or presidents at the "White House," without losing his identity. He is John Van Buren, and nobody else, whether he be sitting cheek-by-jowl with Tom, Dick and Harry at the corner grocery, or debating with the Cokes and Littletons of the law in chancery, or hugging and kissing Queen Victoria in her palace. When the obese, wheezing, antediluvian Hunkers met him in the arena of combat, he attacked them vigorously and repulsed them with great *(s)laughter.*

This apostle of the "young democracy" bids fair to occupy an important niche in the Pantheon of the present time. He has a philosophical and penetrating mind, which has had the advantages and disadvantages of every degree of cultivation — in the palace of the President and in the pothouse of the demagogue. He knows there are zealots, bigots, and earnest Christians in our churches, true patriots and truckling sycophants in our political parties, devoted philanthropists and hollow-hearted pretenders in our benevolent associations, and he governs himself accordingly. He knows the man-about-town, and permits him to be on sociable terms, for that comports with his idea of republicanism. He allows the hackman, the bar-tender, the wood-sawyer and the butcher-boy to call him Jack, and slap him on the shoulder, for the same reason the sportsman plays with his dogs at the commencement of the chase.

John Van Buren is fond of the chase, and he will hunt the rats to the barn, and then set the buildings on fire, for he is truly a "barnburner." Sometimes he has to contend with eloquent reasoners and men of imperious talent. On such occasions he displays great versatility of mind, searching analysis, nice taste, sound judgment, vivid fancy, polished scorn and convincing logic. He can be comic, dramatic, energetic, picturesque, sedate, seductive, inductive, and deductive. He punished Croswell (a political editor) over the remains of Silas Wright, as Marc Antony did Brutus over the dead body of Cæsar; and when the man of "mighty pens" attempted to retreat, he got his "foot in the grating."

At a mass meeting when Prince John was the mouthpiece of his party, one of the "unterrified" proposed three cheers for Cass. "Oh, do n't," said the waggish orator, with a look of mock gravity; "it will be like whistling at a funeral." His speeches are often enlivened with caustic wit and unmistakable homethrusts. Sometimes he leads his hearers through a dead level of political history, without either song or story to change the dull monotony and cheer the impatient hearer. He writes clearly and forcibly, regardless of finish or ornament; has as much shrewdness, adroitness, and world-wisdom as his father, but less secretiveness, less suavity and less dignity; can excel his father at stump speaking, but cannot equal him in writing a message. John annihilates his enemies by the simoon of his sarcasm; his father catches them in the trap of stratagem, and compliments them into bosom friendship. Indeed, he is an unconverted Paul, pursuing (not persecuting) hunkers (not Christians) to strange cities, while his father is Absolom, (without the locks,) winning the hearts of the people.

Prince John is a favorite among the ladies. It is currently reported that when Queen Victoria presented her lily-white hand for him to kiss, according to court etiquette, he, in the face of such usages, with republican gallantry folded his arms around her neck and gave her a hearty smack upon her cheek. It is also said that during his widower-hood he paid some attention to a lady of fortune in Western New York, and once upon a time, when they were riding on horseback, he ventured to pop the question. The lady changed the subject by asking him to overtake her, at the same time giving the horse a hint which caused him to bound forward with the speed of the wind. John was astride a livery stable hack, and was soon distanced, and not a little mortified at seeing the lady's glove upon the road! If it be true that this distinguished "son of York" has refrained from the use of wine, there is a brilliant future before him. He is so frank, so generous, and so gifted, he is the man the people will delight to honor; but he must not, like Alcibiades, deface the images of the gods and expect to be pardoned on the score of eccentricity.

Mr. Van Buren is one of the first men in the "Empire State." He sustains the same relationship to the Democratic party that Seward holds to the Whig party. In personal appearance, he is a tall, spare man, with a "locofocoish" look, somewhat round-shouldered, and stoops a little when he walks, as though he had to bear upon his back the responsibility of the party he lately rejuvinated. His head is prematurely bald, and the scanty supply of hair that is left is soft, thin, and of a foxy color, and has that phosphorescent appearance which indicates a readiness to blaze the moment there is any friction of brain — hence his flashes of wit when he is rubbed. He is about forty years of age, has an ample forehead, expressive eyes, and a countenance denoting a high order of intellect.

He is an eminent lawyer, a great statesman, a progress politician. There is a sort of do n't-care-a-copper-ativeness about him, a reckless spirit of dare-anything-ism, which is repulsive to the amiable, though delightful to the disciples of rowdyism. In his happiest moods, when speaking from the tribune, he is chaste, classical, philosophical, and the *illuminati* become his enthusiastic admirers. He only needs the graceful polish, the serene dignity of his father, added to his other best attributes, to render him one of the most useful, honorable and distinguished men of the nineteenth century.

That he is destined, if his life is spared, to hold an important relation to the politics of this country, is the sincere belief of CRAYON.

WILLIAM A. WHITE.

So long as the writer of these sketches does not belong to the Mutual Admiration Society, and since it has become fashionable for magazine and newspaper publishers to furnish their readers with their own portraits, I can see no earthly nor heavenly reason, why a contributor to the columns of the *New-Englander* may not give to the public a likeness of one of its editors. The readers of this paper have *a right* to see a pen-and-ink daguerreotype of one who talks to them with types so frequently, so plainly, and so eloquently.

WILLIAM A. WHITE is thirty-three years of age, of medium stature and good mould. His temperament is sanguine-nervous, and his development of brain indicates the propelling power he brings to bear upon the reformatory movements to which he is devoted. He has brown hair, which is parted in the middle, leaving a furrow from benevolence to approbativeness. His eyes are blue, complexion fair, face round, fat and plump, indicative of good digestion. The ladies say he would be decidedly handsome, were it not that he disfigures himself by allowing such an overgrowth of moustache, imperial and goatee. I cannot account for his antipathy to razors, for he loves everything else that is *sharp*, and dislikes whatever is *flat*,—which, by-the-way, may be the reason he *cut* some of the grandees of his favorite Order the other day. If he makes them *smart*, he will do more for them than their parents or their schoolmasters have done.

Although Mr. White is a young man, he has been an untiring and unyielding soldier in the ranks of reform, for many years. He is a spontaneous speaker, who can rise in the presence of a regiment of critics, and utter his sentiments unembarrassed, though all the reporters of the press were driving their quills before him. If the Southern "Sons" had not beforehand fitted that gag for the free mouths of the North, they would have found in him a formidable opponent to the obnoxious measure which meets with such unqualified and universal disapprobation wherever humanity is regarded. The magnanimous chivalry of the mighty South, which appears so captivating in history, and so splendid in romance, disappeared on this occasion and looked like Falstaff—great, swaggering and afraid of nothing but danger. There was not a man from the slave side of Mason and Dixon's line, who could have stood before our subject in debate. It is strange that men who have whipped so many blacks were afraid to face one *White*.

As I have intimated, the senior editor of the *New-Englander* is a fluent and forcible speaker. He speaks better than he writes. He is an enthusiast in reform, and manifests but little patience with wooden-head conservatives, who will not comprehend what they cannot count with their fingers, nor measure anything that is longer than a yard-stick. With such men, and with the oppressors of our race, whether they use rum or the raw-hide, liquor or the lash, the cat or the can, he has no fellowship. When he writes about them, his pen foams at the nib; when he speaks about them, his speeches "remind us of some rivers that are sweet in their source, but bitter at the mouth."

Mr. White lacks concentrativeness. He is apt to fly from one subject to another. He needs a balance-wheel. What Kleber said of Napoleon may be said of him: — "He had two faults, that of advancing without considering how he should retreat, and of seizing without considering how he should retain." When convinced that he is right, he has a sort of dare-demon energy, and, like Luther, would go to the Diet of Worms to-day were he sure the worms would diet on him to-morrow. He is impulsive, but his heart is so near his head that his intuition is often a better guide than the matured judgment of some men of greater pretensions. A flash of lightning is sometimes of more service in the dark, than the slow moon which may not rise from behind the cloud in time to avert the danger.

Mr. White has had the advantages of a classical education, and his distinguished brother-in-law, James Russell Lowell, the great poet, was one of his classmates in college. He studied law but practiced the gospel, and, of course, relinquished that profession. Although connected, like Wendell Phillips and Edmund Quincy, with some of the first families in New England, he cheerfully and modestly identifies himself with the progress parties, whom the Pharisees and Sadducees of this generation do not delight to honor. Doubtless he is fond of fame, but he will not sacrifice his sentiments to obtain it; like Cato, he would rather have posterity inquire why no statues were erected to him than why they were.

EDWIN H. CHAPIN.

EDWIN H. CHAPIN is one of the ablest and most eloquent expounders and defenders of the doctrine of unlimited salvation. He has no faith in the old black fellow who keeps the fire-office. He imagines that poets and divines give him more credit for sagacity and potency than he deserves, and that if he ever was a genius he is now in his dotage, and furthermore, that he has not goodness enough to be entitled to our respect, nor influence sufficient over our future destiny to alarm our fears. To him a devil by any other name is just as dreadful, and the Satan he endeavors to subdue he calls Evil, Sin, Crime, Vice, Error. He thinks the distillery, where the worm dieth not and the fires are unquenched, is a hell on earth which causes weeping, wailing and gnashing of teeth.

Mr. Chapin is an independent, straight-forward man, who has a will and a way of his own, and he is willing to allow others the same freedom he assumes himself. He does not expect his church to cough when he takes cold, nor to acquiesce in silent submission to every proposition that he makes. He is not a theological tyrant, threatening vengeance, and outer-darkness, and eternal fire, to all the members of his flock who will not uncomplainingly and unhesitatingly yield to his spiritual supervisorship. His lessons and lectures may sometimes smell of the lamp, but they never smell of brimstone. His education, his temperament, his organization of brain, his natural benevolence, and the society in which he has lived, moved, and had his being, have contributed to make him a preacher of the gospel. He advocates with heroic courage and untiring zeal the doctrines of his faith, but is universally respected by all denominations of professing Christians.

Mr. Chapin is happily constituted. The animal and the angel of his nature are so nicely balanced, and his poetical temperament is so admirably controlled by his practical knowledge, that his intellectual efforts are invariably stamped with the mint-mark of true currency. There is harmonious blending of the poetical and the practical, a pleasant union of the material with the spiritual, an arm-in-arm connection of the ornamental and useful, a body and soul joined together in his discourses. He avoids two extremes, and is not so material as to be clodish, of the earth earthy, nor so ærial as to be vapory or of the clouds cloudy. There is something tangible, solid, nutritious and enduring, in his sermons. He is not profound in the learning of the schools. Many of his inferiors could master him on doctrinal questions. The outbursting and overwhelming effusions of his natural eloquence, the striking originality of his conceptions, the irresistible power of his captivating voice, the vivid and copious display of illustration, thrill and charm the appreciative hearer. He presents his arguments and appeals with an articulation as distinct and understandable as his gesticulation is awkward. He is sometimes abrupt, rapid and vehement, but never "tears a passion to tatters." "His tenacious memory enables him to quote with great promptitude, and he has that delicate, sensitive taste which enables him to select, with unerring precision, whatever is truly sublime and beautiful."

Mr. Chapin declaims splendidly, in spite of his hands, which are always in his way. The stiff and technical restraints of style, which disfigure the pulpit efforts of some divines, never appear in his sermons, but seem rather to pinion his elbows and cramp his fingers. He has a fervid imagination, great facility of expression, is scrupulously correct in his pronunciation; never indulges in hypocritical cant. There is no theatrical uplifting of the hands and uprolling of the eyes, so frequently witnessed in the hysteric raptures of mahogany orators. He seems to have a thorough knowledge of his subject, and commands your admiration by the kingly majesty and sublime beauty of his thought. Now he flings a page of meaning into a single aphorism, — now he electrifies his spell-bound hearers with a spontaneous burst of eloquence, — now he dissolves their eyes to tears by a wizard stroke of pathos, — now he controls their hearts with the sovereign power of a monarch who rules the mind-realm. "He infuses his soul into his voice, and both into the nerves and heart of the hearer."

In person, he is stout, fleshy and well-proportioned. He has a full, florid face, which indicates good health and happy contentment; countenance mild, benignant and thoughtful, with an expresion of integrity, denoting his inability to perform a mean action; is near-sighted, and this defect is no small disadvantage to him when he reads, and may account for his ungraceful action in the pulpit, since it compels him to face his manuscript so closely he almost eats his own words and salutes his own rich figures and glowing sentiments, and fulfils literally the scripture maxim, "He shall kiss his own lips who giveth a correct answer." As I have just intimated, he usually reads his discourses, although he is an easy extemporaneous speaker; but he is apt to become so intensely excited he rarely trusts to his impulses. He commands a very ready pen, and is the author of two or three small volumes, which are widely circulated. His hair is dark brown. He wears glasses, so I cannot tell the color of his eyes; has a broad, high forehead, indicating the intellectual strength of its owner; is about forty-five years of age, and has labored with honor and success for many years, in Richmond, Va., Charlestown, Mass., as well as Boston, but is now preaching in the city of New York, where he is very popular and useful.

I must be pardoned the mention of one fault. He is careless, sometimes slovenly, in his dress, which is not owing to a lack of taste, but to the fact that his studies absorb his time and attention. Since he has possessed a "better-half," there has been less manifestation of this disagreeable trait.

CHARLES C. BURLEIGH.

Charles C. Burleigh, the eccentric and eloquent abolitionist, is brother to William H. and George Burleigh, the celebrated poets. He is an out and out "come-outer"— a non-compromising radical — a splendid scholar — an off-hand orator. He is not so genial as Garrison — but has more force — not so bitter as Pillsbury, but his severity has a keener edge and cuts deeper — less eloquent than Phillips but more logical than he — not so blunt as Foster, but like him, he is a plain-dealer. His best thoughts are struck out at a heat, and come to the heart winged with words of fire. There is thunder and lightning in his logic — and the concussion, as well as the conclusion, are irresistible. His arguments are not betinselled with gauze and silver spangles; it is pure gold that glitters in his speeches. You look in vain for the double refined essence of nonsense and affectation with which literary dandies perfume their productions. There is a smell of gunpowder in the atmosphere, and a mighty fluttering of game, when he levels his gun at a multitude. His arguments are forcible — his appeals pathetic — his language classical. When he follows an opponent in debate, he begins at the beginning, pursues his meanderings, and sweeps away his sophistry as gossamer is swept by the wind. He may be seen selling books at the door of the building where the convention is held, one minute, and the next minute he may be seen on the platform, addressing an audience — unmoved by the cat-calls in the gallery, or the scribbling of the reporters at his elbow. He speaks right on, as though, like the prophet Ezekiel, he had swallowed the parchment roll. There is no flaw in his unpremeditated addresses — you cannot discover any welding marks. I do not set him up "too steep," when I venture the assertion that his addresses found in the abolition papers, will compare favorably with the best speeches made in the Senate Chamber at Washington. Notwithstanding his superior talents and his surpassing power of language, he is a wild man, who ought to be caught and shaved, for his beard stands, or rather hangs, in the way of his usefulness. Unlike Samson, his weakness is in his hair, and he could better slay the Philistines and shake the pillars of the temple, if he would permit some one to crop off his locks. The first time the writer saw him, he looked like a madman just out of Bedlam — but he spoke like an Apostle whose lips had been touched with a live coal from the altar of Inspiration. I have seen him frequently since that time, and think that he looks better than he formerly did — as for his speaking, his last effort is always the best.

Mr. Burleigh is a tall, thin man, with light eyes that glow and sparkle when he speaks. He wears a golden beard, long enough to please the taste of the most fastidious Nazarite; permits his hair on his head to grow long, parts it in the middle, and it rolls in auburn ringlets over his narrow shoulders; dresses plainly, and gives abundant proof that dame Fashion seldom or never replenishes his wardrobe. Is somewhat inclined to Quakerism — although his creed does not appear in the brim of his beaver or the cut of his coat. His character is irreproachable. He has labored untiringly for the welfare of humanity since he and Theodore Weld, and a band of kindred spirits, broke loose from Lane Seminary.

WILLIAM H. SEWARD.

SENATOR SEWARD is the Daniel O'Connell of America; not in stature, for the former is *petit* — the latter was prodigious; not in wit, for the Yankee seldom perpetrates even a pun, while the Irishman was a "book in breeches," and every page gleaming with wit; not in eloquence, for Seward requires preparation and speaks without much unction. O'Connell spoke spontaneously, and every word was a throb; not in faith, for the defender of the "higher law" is almost a Protestant, while the Great Agitator, as all know, was altogether a Catholic. Yet there is a resemblance, notwithstanding their dissimilarities. Seward stands at the tip top of his profession as a lawyer, and so did O'Connell. Seward made a sensation in the American Senate; O'Connell did the same in the House of Commons. Seward identifies himself with the party of Freedom. O'Connell hated slavery, and "oppression made that wise man mad." Seward is charged with demagogueism. O'Connell made himself all things to some men that he might gain some. Seward has won the sympathies of the masses and is the pet of the liberty-loving people of the North. O'Connell was the idol of Ireland, and his memory will ever live in the hearts of his countrymen. Seward is dreaded as much by the Old Hunkers of this country, as O'Connell was feared by the tyrant

Tories of Great Britain. Seward split the Whig party; so did O'Connell. Seward is a practical temperance man; O'Connell was a pledged tee-totaller. Seward would like to be President of the United States; O'Connell desired to be King of Ireland. Seward is a great man among great men. He is not so volcanic as Benton,—not so logical as Webster, —not so eloquent as Clay,—not so brittle as Foote,—not so jovial as Hale; but he can write a better letter than any of them. A little from his pen will go a great distance and keep a long time. His classic style, his earnest air, his truthful manner, his uncommon sense, his perfect self-control, his thorough knowledge of the leading questions of the day, compel the attention and admiration of the hearer. He is never timid, never tame, never squeamish, never vulgar, never insulting. He is independent without egotism, modest without subserviency, dignified without pomposity, and sociable without affectation.

We need look back but a few months to find much to admire in the character of Seward. See him rise in the Senate Chamber, and hear him defend the rights of humanity in an atmosphere of opposing influences. There sits the imperious Clay, with flushed face and flashing eyes — and the Great Expounder, with pouting lip and brow of thunder; and fiery Foote, phosphorescent with excitement; and philosophical Cass, as placid as though the Union was not in danger. He (Seward) drops a word in defence of the higher law, and forthwith there is "ground and lofty tumbling." The enraged Senators appear to think that regard for the Commandments is an insult to the Constitution — that reverence for the Deity is "renegadism" from duty. So they examine the elements of nature, analyze the facts in history, and pervert the truths of the Bible, to prove that we ought to obey men rather that to obey God. Had Seward been an ordinary man, he would have been swamped amid the storm; but he remained firm as a rock in the midst of that stormy sea, and gave proof, that, although minimum in person, he was maximum in power. Their impotent threats could no more shake his resolution, than a pinch of snuff could make him sneeze, (excuse the homely illustration,) for the former went in at his ears almost as frequently as the latter does into his nostrils.

Governor Seward, as he is called, is a little past the prime of life, somewhat under the common stature, has a very large head, with a few grey hairs playing hide and seek amid the mass of light brown; he has blue eyes, a small forehead, a long nose, and a patrician mouth. He is well to do in the world, happy in his domestic relations, enjoys a glorious reputation, and his star is still in the ascendant.

DANIEL WEBSTER.

AMERICA is the greatest continent, and embraces within its limits the grandest mountains, the broadest lakes, the longest rivers, the largest prairies, and with all these, the mightiest *intellect.* Its mountains stand up like pillars supporting the azure arch in the temple of nature; its lakes are inland seas; its rivers could swallow the waters of Europe without overflowing their banks; and its mind is correlative with the magnificence of its scenery. There is but one Niagara, and that is in America; there is but one Webster, and he is in America. The cataract flows now, as it did when God first smote the rock in this Western wilderness, and He has woven a rainbow about its silver forehead, and crowned it with a fountain of diamonds. It shouts the same song of liberty it did when the world was in its infancy. It is free and mighty, and cannot be hushed into silence, nor flattered into subserviency. So with Webster, when he lifts up his voice for freedom, it is like "deep calling unto deep;" and the light of Heaven illuminates his magnetic eyes and beams on his mighty forehead.

Geologists have discovered the colossal bones of the Mastodon, and hence we infer that there were larger animals in ages gone by, than we have living at present; so, future historians will find, in their mutilated and mouldy libraries, the remains of Webster's greatness. In the glory of his manhood he represented Massachusetts; defended liberty; sympathized with humanity, and won the approbation of all good men. In the arena of debate he usually came off more than conqueror. He was regarded as *the* Senator of the United States. When he rose in his place, in the Council Chamber of the nation, with a voice of thunder and eyes on fire, every face was turned toward him, every tongue was silent, for he was clad to the teeth in armor, had a spear like a weaver's beam, and had been trained to battle. He has great self-possession, coolness, adroitness and tact; never was remarkable for sunshiny gaiety of imagination; rarely strayed to select bright flowers in the garden of literature; his attempts at wit were like the antics of the elephant that tried to mimic the lap-dog; but he was emphatically great. He was the defender of the Constitution, and could present arguments in its defence with irrestible force and eloquence. His words were full of marrow, his logic unctuous with fatness. He defeated his opponents, not by the "delicacy of his tact, but by the prodigious power of his reason." There "was no honied paste of poetic diction" encrusting his speeches, "like the candied coat of the auricula," but there was tremendous weight in his arguments.

Webster, in earlier days, was sublime as Chatham, classical as Burke, terse as Macintosh, forcible as Tully. Endowed, by nature, with a noble and commanding person, he never failed to attract attention. When excited in debate, his granite face glowed with intellect; "the terrors of his beak, the lightnings of his eye, were insufferable." He was the king of the Senate, for nature had stamped him with the unmistakable mark of sovereignty, regardless of the republicanism of his country. There was grace in his gesture, dignity in his deportment, and humanity as well as patriotism in his speeches. His voice was rich, full, and clear; now thrilling like the blast of a trumpet, now intimidating by the awful solemnity of its tone, now animating by its soul-stirring notes. Abroad, he was the lion of London, his noble exterior making him "a man of mark." He has coal-black hair, (now thickly sprinkled with grey,) a lofty brow, "the forge of thought;" magnificent eyes; an ample chest; a patrician hand; a face broad and dark as some of the fugitives he would return to bondage. See him in the zenith of his manhood, standing on the battle-ground at Bunker Hill, with kingly dignity, uttering sentiments that will be fresh in the memories of millions, when the shaft of granite now standing there shall have crumbled to dust! Apparently as impregnable as the granite hills of his own New Hampshire, who supposed that he, so great and gifted, towering above ordinary men, was as the mountain which wraps the cloud-cloak about its shoulders, while a vest of eternal snow keeps the sunshine forever from its heart! The mountain is great, sublime and lofty, but cold, barren and unapproachable; it points toward Heaven, but remains fixed to earth.

Daniel Webster has accomplished noble feats, for which he merits the gratitude of good men. Since the days of Washington, there has been no man so well qualified, in many points, for the presidency, as he. His impatience and irritability, in consequence of his disappointment, have been frequently exhibited. As a last resort, he has tried to conciliate the South at the expense of the North. As a public speaker, he seldom enlivens his arguments with flashes of wit, but he has said some keen things, which have become as common as "household words." At a public meeting, a young aspirant for poetical and political honors attempted to drink a toast to the honor of the immortal John Q. Adams, who was present. "Mr. Adams," said the toaster, "may he perplex his enemies as" —— here the speaker hesitated, and Webster thundered out, "as he has his friends." Foote made a fulsome speech in praise of Mr. Webster, at one time, in the Senate, but the "god-like" cut him short by shouting "*Git eöut.*" The Yankee twang he gave the sentence convulsed the Senate with irrepressible laughter.

For superior specimens of pure style, lofty reasoning and eloquent declamation, read Mr. Webster's arguments before the Supreme Court, his speeches delivered in Faneuil Hall, his best efforts in the Senate Chamber, his unstudied responses at public dinners and conventions, his lectures before the lyceums, his remarks on the great political and constitutional questions of the past and present times. Indeed, all are familiar with these efforts of a master mind. The professional skill and the parliamentary talent of Mr. Webster are appreciated on both sides of the Atlantic. He has contended with the ablest intellects, — stout competitors, keen opponents, — and always came off with flying colors, when he was in the right. Even his rivals give him the credit of being the most forcible debater in America.

At the age of thirty he appeared in the Congress of 1812, and Mr. Lowndes then said of him, that the North had not his equal, nor the South his superior. That he has been a sagacious statesman, a skillful diplomatist, a profound investigator, and the greatest thinker in America, is the opinion of millions of his countrymen.

CHARLES SUMNER.

NEW YORK is the head-quarters of commerce, a great wilderness of marble and mortar, the abode of merchant princes and millionaires. Its harbor is crowded with ships from every nation, its mammoth mercantile establishments contain every variety of fabric and produce, its streets are busy as a broken ant-heap, its spires point, like fingers of pilgrims, to the land of the beautiful above, and its grog-shops are plentiful as carbuncles on the face of the toper. It has the best editors, and the poorest speakers, of any city in the Union. Philadelphia is noted for handsome buildings erected on straight lines. It is the metropolis of magazine-dom, where Graham and Godey make gold and win golden honors. It is famed for the brotherly love of its inhabitants, which trait is beautifully displayed in the manner in which they get up rows and send their fellow-citizens to Heaven. Boston is the bank of New England, the beacon-light of reform, the seat of science and learning, the forum of chaste, classical, thrilling, heart-quaking, soul-stirring eloquence. There is no city in the United States that contains so much speaking talent as Boston. Baltimore is choleric, noisy, and patriotic; Philadelphia is fastidious, lymphatic, and metaphysical; Washington is like Babel, where there is a confusion of languages, or like a vineyard of lazy laborers, where there is a *winey* atmosphere ; New York is energetic, bombastic, and original ; Cincinnati is slow of speech, but sound at the heart. Boston is radical, forcible, eloquent.

Among the most eminent speakers in the modern Athens, Charles Sumner stands preëminently conspicuous, for the classic elegance of his style, the Protean power of his thought, and the finished beauty of his illustrations. He is one of the most remarkable men of this remarkable age, and favorable circumstances have rendered him the darling favorite of good fortune. He was cradled in Faneuil Hall, Judge Story was his teacher, and Harvard University the school in which he was taught. When he had availed himself of the advantages afforded by this institution of learning, he made the tour of Europe. England, France and Germany contributed liberally to his store of knowledge. If he has not an ample competence, he has what is better — an army of friends and a thorough education.

Charles Sumner is a stockholder in the bank of original thought. We may know he has considerable bullion there, for his drafts are honored at sight, and our first men are his endorsers. He has great power of condensation, without the wearisome monotony which often accompanies the writings and sayings of close thinkers and rigid reasoners. There is a vigorous and graceful stateliness, an easy felicity, a fastidious accuracy and an imperial dignity in his style, which is both commanding and fascinating. There is a vast breadth of comprehension and a vast depth of meaning in his matter. There is also a luminous beauty, a Gothic grandeur, a sublime gorgeousness, in his labored and polished essays, which entitle them to the appellation of prose poems. He sometimes invests his ideas in such lively, such attractive, such speaking, such *magic* language, and displays so much philosophical sagacity, so much poetical sensibility, so much profound knowledge of ecclesiastical and political history, the reader and the listener are carried away on the current, while they are admiring, almost adoring, the man whose kindling words have set their imaginations on fire.

Mr. Sumner's orations are written with great care. They abound with allusions to the sayings and doings of the ancients, and manifest deep research and profound thought. His brilliant arguments at the bar have elicited unbounded admiration, and his model manner of delivery enhances the value of his eloquent appeals. The dreary desert of a common case is sure to bloom with garden beauty under his management. The forum, however, is his *forte*. He has the dignity of Pitt, without his pompous declamation; the sublimity of Burke, without his tedious uniformity; the vigor of Fox, without his roughness. He is not so fluent as the first, not so classical as the second, not so ready and original as the third. He has more solidity but less eloquence than Phillips; more energy but less originality than Mann; more poetry and as much polish as Everett. His heart is not an island, separated from his head, but a peninsula, uniting one with the other. There is a relationship between the throb of the former and the thought of the latter. There is a joining of impulse and intellect. The affections and the reflections are brothers and sisters. The heart thinks and feels, the head feels and thinks.

In this respect Mr. Sumner differs from not a few distinguished men. Sumner believes in Christian law, and throws the weight of his influence, the force of his example, and the skill of his profession, in the scale of the right and true. He is a preacher of peace, a lover of freedom, a worker for prison amelioration — in short, a noble soldier in the ranks of reform. With a generous, impulsive nature, he feels the woes and sufferings of every portion of the human family.

Charles Sumner is a popular man. The masses admire him because there is no "dough" in his face, no demagogueism in his politics. The turncoats, flunkeys, time-servers, office-seekers, and political hypocrites of every party, fear him as the enemies of Greece did the Athenian orator, but they cannot despise him, they cannot ostracise him, they cannot make him false to his convictions. Hence he is the man the people delight to honor, though he seeks no popular applause. He is now in the prime of manhood, and the star of his fame is in the ascendant. In person, he is tall, well-proportioned, with a low but broad forehead, light magnetic eyes, and a luxuriant growth of dark brown hair. He has a long, uneven face, which is marked with the manly traits for which he is distinguished. His smile is very sunny and infectious, and his greeting very cordial; walks with firmness, and swings his arms (especially when upon the platform) as though he designed to knock down the obstacles in his way; has a full, rich bass voice, which becomes very seductive as he proceeds in his speech, enlisting irresistibly the attention, and appealing warmly to the feelings. When he is intensely excited, the tones of his voice move one like the blast of a bugle. As an orator, he has but few superiors.

Mr. Sumner would excel as a diplomatist, for he has that peculiar ingenuity and intuitive skill which would enable him to disentangle the complicated questions that would come before him for arbitrament. When his party desire to move the political world they are apt to shift it upon his Atlantean shoulders. Is there a great gulf between Dives the demagogue, and Lazarus of his own league?—*He* will bridge over the chasm, if it can be done, and unite them in mutual friendship, without sacrificing truth and right on the altar of compromise. But some say Mr. Sumner is not sufficiently *practical.* He hopes to see the dawn of a golden future, and mistakes the scintillating lights of the Northern skies for the sunrise of the millennial day. Although he is ambitious in worthy causes, he is wise, and patiently bides his time, without egotistically thrusting himself before the people; is fond of fame, but when he is crowned with honors his modesty is equal to his gratitude. Has a Faneuil-Hall-full of affectionate admirers in his own city, and multitudes of them elsewhere.

As might be expected from his heart-sympathies, Mr. Sumner early connected himself with the Free Soil party; indeed, was one of its originators,—and without question is one of the ablest men in it—and politicians of all shades of opinion will agree that that party embodies a large share of intellectual, moral and personal strength. Recent events in the political affairs of Massachusetts have placed Mr. Sumner conspicuously before the community as a candidate for the United States Senate.* If he should receive the honor of that post, he would be more of a statesman than a partisan, more of a sound, humane, political economist than the mouth-piece of a faction—and I need not say, would do honor to the State he represents. His benevolence of character never will allow him to be a party demagogue, but for all that gives dignity to manhood or exalts true political science, he has every requisite.

MOSES GRANT.

Moses Grant has obtained a world-wide celebrity, by his untiring efforts to ameliorate the condition of the unfortunate children of poverty and sorrow. The widow and the orphan have reason to rise up and call him blessed. The drunkard and the prisoner have abundant cause to remember him gratefully, for his labors of love. Although advanced in years, he has the vigor, forecast and decision of the prime of life. Between the hours of eight and one, in the morning, he may be found every working-day in his office, serving the poor. Groups of men, women and children, of every complexion, from every country, may be seen at his office every forenoon, soliciting aid and advice. The dusky African, the mercurial Celt, the stolid Englishman, the chattering Frenchman, the lymphatic German, and the exiled Hungarian. One sits on a bench at the window, eating a bowl of soup — another stoops down to fit a pair of shoes to his feet — another strips the rags from his back and puts on a warm jacket. Look at the procession passing through the gate. Here is a boy with a bag of rice, there is a girl with a loaf of bread, yonder is a woman with a basket of provisions. See that red-faced young man,— his home is in the country, but he last night fell among thieves, between Broad and Beacon streets, and he has just borrowed a sum sufficient to take him to his parents. That modest woman, so plainly yet so neatly dressed, suffered uncomplainingly until pinching hunger compelled her to solicit charity — her immediate wants are supplied, and employment will be procured for her. The man with a slouched hat and seedy coat has signed the pledge, and left his brandy bottle among the curiosities in the Deacon's temperance museum. There comes the porter with a stack of letters and papers from the post-office — the former will be answered and the latter examined, before the rising of to-morrow's sun.

It is now noon. The sad faced, broken-hearted, and down-trodden procession, has passed away from the beautiful residence, and the owner and occupant of the mansion hurries down to his place of business, from that to the bank, and then home again, in time to dine. After dinner he calls for his carriage and takes a poor boy to the Farm School — dropping in at South Boston to see the juvenile offenders, and calling, on his return, to see a sick woman, and administer such consolation and assistance as he can render. Her lips are white as the wild white rose, but she calls for blessings to descend upon kind friends whose visits are better than medicine to her aching frame and her breaking heart.

The subject of this sketch is never idle. Now presiding at a Mass Meeting on the Common, or in Faneuil Hall, or in Tremont Temple — then making a speech to the convicts in Charlestown Prison, or visiting the paupers at Deer Island — or attending to his official business at the Board of Aldermen — or his duties as an office bearer in the Brattle Street Church, where his father served before him, in the same capacity of Deacon.

His father was one of the brave men who threw the tea overboard in Boston harbor. Mr. Grant is the senior partner in a large paper establishment, Overseer of the Poor,

Almoner for the benevolent who choose to contribute of their abundance for the relief of the distressed; President of the Boston Temperance Society, and a Director in many other institutions. He is a man of fortune, has a good education, and has visited Europe. He writes a sensible letter, and makes a practical speech; is peculiarly happy in his remarks to children, and always a welcome visitor at all juvenile demonstrations. For many years he has been identified with the temperance cause. His house, and purse, and heart, are ever open for the advancement of his favorite enterprise. He is the unfaltering friend and patron of that eminent orator, J. B. Gough, and stood by his side in the hour of trial, when summer friends forsook him.

It is rather difficult to describe his person. The portrait in the American Temperance Magazine is a pretty fair resemblance, although not a perfect likeness. He has brown hair—sprinkled with lines of silver—blue eyes, thin face, cheeks somewhat sunken, is rather under the medium size. He is of the nervous-sanguine temperament; has a singular habit of twitching the muscles of his face and shrugging his shoulders when excited; often speaks abruptly, when pressed with business, and does not always appear to the best advantage at first sight, but wears well and "improves on acquaintance." In a word, he is a man of sound judgment, superior business talents, a practical philanthropist, and a sincere Christian. For many years he has been a hero in the battle-field of life, and many would be willing to give a dukedom to possess such green laurels and golden honors as he has won.

JOHN B. GOUGH.

THE snow-storm last Sunday prevented many from attending meetings of worship. Even the saloons were not so well patronized as usual. The descending snow covered the footsteps of the unfortunate victims of appetite, as though the flakes had been angels of mercy spreading out their white wings to obliterate the way to ruin. Notwithstanding the inclemency of the weather, and the untravellable condition of the streets, multitudes of men, women and children are wending their way to the Tremont Temple. Who is the magnet of attraction? What is his theme? Is it the novelty of a new comer that brings out the masses on such a night? No; the orator J. B. Gough, has spoken more than twelve dozen times on that same subject in the same place. Is it his profound learning that enables him to invest such a question with so much interest? No; he is an uneducated man. Is he the originator or leader of a clique or party, or does he occupy an elevated position in the political world, that he commands so much influence? No; he does not publicly indentify himself with any political party. He was formerly intemperate, and occupied an humble position in the ranks of the lowly poor. See him, and hear him, and you will then know why he fills the Temple, and, like Samson, shakes it afterwards. He is not a reasoner. He is not a philosopher. He is not a scholar. Look at his magnetic eyes—and the light beaming on his pale forehead. Hear the silvery tones of his thrilling voice. See how off-handish he is. He rises from his seat as though he supposed nobody was looking at him. With his hands folded behind him, he walks to the front of the platform, and announces the number of times he has spoken in the city. Speaks lowly and slowly at first, but the color that comes like a flash over his face, now and then advertises the uprush of blood to the brain. Now he has cut loose from his moorings, and is fairly out at sea. Every sail is set; the wind is fair; the ocean is smooth or rough, as he may choose to make it, for God has given him power to raise the storm, and power to bid the waves be still. Every hearer is attentive. The great flood of faces, up-turned and side-turned, indicate the interest. No one leaves, unless it is some unappreciating dull-head—or some one whose business or indisposition demands him to absent himself. The orator stops not to round his periods, or polish his sentences. He is an actor, as well as an orator, and could excel as a pantomime player.

I know of no man living who can tell a story better than he. All who hear him once are anxious to hear him again. What a graphic description he has just given of Felix McConnell! We see the plague-spot on his face—the blood oozing from the ends of his bursting fingers, and gushing from the gaping wound, out of which his soul has fled. Now he tells a tale of pity, and women weep like children; and strong men, "albeit unused to the melting mood," brush away the tears shyly, as though it were a sin to shed them. Now he relates a ludicrous story, and laughter shakes the tear-drops from fair faces, as the Summer wind sweeps the dew from flowers. He has been with his brethren and sisters around the communion table, to-day, and he came here with a heart full of love to God and good will to man. His white-haired and venerable father sits behind, on the platform, and seems deeply interested in the address. Deacon Grant, his unfaltering friend, is also present. It is a stormy night — the lights burn dimly — and the meeting would be a dull affair, were it not for the electric eloquence of the speaker.

This is his farewell speech, and it is one of his happiest efforts. What a thrilling description he has just given, of a man in a boat, going over the Falls of Niagara! We see the bed of the river, above the rapids, as smooth as molten silver. The boat glides on; hands beckon and voices call, from the shore, for the man to stop — but he laughs, and replies that he will "hard up" the helm and pull on his oars in time. The birds sing, the flowers bloom — a rainbow is woven on the forehead of the water yonder, and a shower of liquid diamonds descend in the sun-light. Now the boat approaches the rapids! — The unhappy man grasps the oars — the veins on his forehead stand out like whipcords — the beaded sweat rolls like rain down his face. Now the boat and the man are swallowed by one wave and disgorged by another! — Now all is lost, for ever lost!

Mr. Gough bids his hearers farewell again, — alluding to the time when he was an actor, in the same building (then the Tremont Theatre) where he now advocates the cause of temperance.

Some who read this may like to know something about the personal appearance of Mr. Gough. He is thirty-five years of age, of slender build and of medium stature. His temperament is nervous-bilious; hair dark, with here and there a line of silver in it; and his long, pale, thin face is lit up with a pair of large electric eyes. Hard drinking, before his reform, and hard work since, have creased his brow with furrows, and left the print of the "crows'-feet," at the corners of his eyes. He dresses neatly, in plain black. The writer knows, from personal and intimate acquaintance, that he is not only a gifted man, but, to use a common-place expression — a good fellow.

The writer heard him on another occasion, when he complained of being tired and travel-worn, and appeared dull and sleepy. When his name was announced, he rose rather awkwardly and walked leisurely toward the foot-lights, with his hands folded behind him, and commenced speaking slowly, in a low tone of voice. In a few moments, however, the lightning began to flash from his eyes, and the thunder of eloquence to peal from his tongue, while his face shone with the inspiration of his genius. He treated his hearers to outbursts of pathos, inimitable humor, pungent wit, and thrilling facts. It was one of his mightest efforts, and was driven home to the heart with such force as to make a life-lasting impression.

Mr. Gough's speeches are disjointed, and lack that solidity which characterizes the speeches of some of the great pioneers in the temperance cause; but he is emphatically the man for the million. Since the day of the lamented Summerfield, no man has attracted so much attention and won so much admiration as he. Gough is generous, frank, and sociable, fond of sport, and enjoys a rough-and-tumble game of innocent fun, as well as any one.

Altogether, he is a remarkable man, and has been instrumental in accomplishing incalculable good. His eloquence reminds one of the onward flow of sweeping waters. The silver thread unwinding from a hidden spring in the mountain falls lightly at first, but gathers volume and voice as it proceeds, until it murmurs in the brooklet, shouts in the torrent, thunders in the cataract, and rolls on in beauty, glory, majesty and sublimity in the river, and finally swells the waves of the mighty ocean.

LEWIS CASS.

Hon. Lewis Cass is a gallant General, a good citizen, an eminent statesman, who has served his country at home and abroad, for many years, with honor to himself and credit to his country. He is a man of unimpeachable purity of character, — and his abstemious habits (unless he has met with a recent change) deserve the commendation of all good men. He is pugnacious, and often shakes his fist in the face of John Bull; is ambitious, and has made high bids for the presidency. In his efforts to provoke the former and secure the latter, he has displayed his weakest points.

Lewis Cass is a great man — physically and intellectually. There is nothing trashy or inane in his speeches; he is not subject to poetical hysterics, and there is not much of the majestic or the sublime in his speeches. It is seldom that great and mighty thoughts leap from his mouth, as "Minerva sprang from the brain of Jove;" but he is plain, practical, philosophical, argumentative, correct, and classical. He does not soar like an angel, but he stands erect like a man. He has a well-balanced, ratiocinative mind — deeply experienced, and thoroughly cultivated. He cannot, like Webster, "heap Pelion upon Ossa," until his opponent is overwhelmed and crushed to the dust, — but he digs deeply, until the victim is first undermined, and finally buried under his own *premises.*

He is corpulent — almost gross — and has a dull face; is a perfect gentleman in his address, excellent company, when he is sufficiently acquainted to "unbend the brow," and in the convivial circle he can contribute his share of merriment. He speaks French fluently, and is familiar with other languages. He is a man whom his party delights to honor, — and has been governor, representative, foreign minister, is now senator, and several times he has been almost President of the United States. He lives in a large, plain, democratic-looking house, in the beautiful city of Detroit. He is now ill with the ague* — the only thing that can shake him. Senator Douglass has recently employed an artist to take his portrait. Perhaps he designs to hang the shadow on the wall, and take the place of the substance himself. He is highly esteemed in Michigan, and has more influence there than any other man in the State. Permit me to record a joke, which has been exposed to the sun and air so long it has become dry, if not stale. "Tell Hale," said Cass, "that he is a Granite goose." "Tell Cass," replied Hale, "that he is a Michi-*gander!*"

FRANCIS TUKEY.

FRANCIS TUKEY is the Napoleon of City Marshals.—Lynx-eyed and lion-hearted, keen as a sharper, and brave as a soldier, he displays remarkable skill, tact, force and foresight, when he pursues a criminal, or subdues a mob, or storms a gambling hell. The sight of a dirk or the snap of a pistol never make him absent in body, nor scare away his presence of mind. He is not like the giant of Rabelais, who could swallow windmills one day, and yet choke at the sight of a pat of fresh butter the next, for he never loses that calm, cool self-possession, so requisite in a rogue-catcher. The mantle of Jacob Hays must have fallen upon his shoulders, for when he is in pursuit of the violators of the law, thick walls are transparent, deep schemes are unriddled, and bold villains are brought to justice.

The police force under his management has been so well trained that it can be employed to the best advantage. This civil army can be brought into service on any emergency, at short notice, with all the uniformity and efficiency of a disciplined army.

In our large cities, rascality is reduced to a science. Pockets are picked by rule — merchants are swindled by accomplished financiers — banks are entered by the most *uncivil* engineers — gamblers go dressed like gentlemen — burglars are armed with false keys, bowie-knives and revolvers. Consequently, a Marshal must have the courage of Cromwell, the zeal of Luther, if he would be a terror to such evil-doers, and a praise to those who do well. He must not only have a head to contrive, but a heart to feel, also. He must not be like the man who, because he had passed through the Custom-House, supposed the Government had *taken off the duties* he owed his fellow-citizens. While the guilty must be punished the innocent must be protected.

Marshal Tukey is a native of Maine, by profession a lawyer. He is in the full vigor of manhood, about five feet nine inches in height, of good mould, and his head is phrenologically well developed; his hair smooth, and black as the wing of a raven; eyes large, dark and piercing; face pale, thin and thoughtful; forehead quite intellectual; mouth well cut, and his smile is quite infectious. He has recently connected himself with the Temple of Honor, in this city. He never was habituated to the inordinate use of intoxicating drink — consequently he had no appetite to contend with. He would have united with that noble institution long ago, had it not been for the fact that every disinterested deed performed by a public man is sure to be regarded by the selfish as political manœuvring for place and power.

WILLIAM R. STACY.

William R. Stacy is a plain, business man, whose hands and heart and soul are earnestly engaged in the total abstinence reform. In season and out of season, he is the same untiring, uncompromising and unflinching champion of the cause. In Societies, in Sections, in Divisions, in Tents and in Temples, he is known as an efficient worker. Fair-weather friends and summer-fly advocates of abstinence doctrines are constantly rebuked by his unyielding adherence to the letter and the spirit of the pledge. Temperance thermometers, whose mercury is sure to rise and fall, according to the state of the atmosphere, wonder with open mouths and open eyes, and leathern ears and leaden brains, why Mr. Stacy denies himself the lazy ease which they misname enjoyment. Politicians, who can accommodate themselves to every sect in religion, to every party in politics, to every shade of society, and, like chameleons, assume the color of the community in which they move, are astonished that a man of his tact and influence, and persevering energy, does not attempt to reap laurels and gain gold in the field of political action. Those who need not envy the donkey its redundancy of ear, are surprised that such a sensible man should engage in such "small business."

Captain Stacy is President of the Parent Washingtonian

Temperance Society, in this city — an institution which has been in successful operation for eight years, during which time hundreds and thousands have been added to its membership. This good Samaritan society not only secures names to the pledge, but feeds the hungry, clothes the destitute, visits the sick. It has been instrumental in healing hearts that were broken, and restoring to society men who had degraded themselves by the use of strong drinks. Through Summer and Winter, Spring and Autumn, fair weather and foul weather, Mr. Stacy has attended the meeting of this society.

His friends seem to appreciate his worth by heaping honors upon him. The last two years, he was Most Worthy Associate of the National Division. He is now Most Worthy Templar of the National Temple. These distinctions have fallen upon a worthy man. There is no poetry, no tinselry about his speeches. His thoughts are clad in a thin covering of scanty words. He works noiselessly and out of sight, but very effectually. Is there a cross to carry, *his* shoulders are chosen to bear the burden. Is there money to raise, *his* financiering skill is called into exercise. Is there a mammoth meeting to be held, *he* is expected to make the necessary preparations.

Mr. Stacy is in the prime of life, a man of common stature, has dark hair, large light eyes, an honest face, a good development of benevolence, and firmness enough to render him obstinate when opposed — providing he has reason to believe he is on the right side of the question. Few men are so well acquainted with the "workings" of the National Temple as he; few men have more influence in the great national temperance movement then he. It is evident that he accepts office for the purpose of extending the sphere of his usefulness, and not for the gratification of his personal vanity.

He never occupies much time in his public addresses — does not stop to dissect his dictionary for choice language, but speaks out in manly style the thoughts that are uppermost in his mind. He is not a classical scholar, and never tries to pass for more than he is worth, by awkward attempts at rounding periods and polishing sentences. His striking characteristics are generosity, energy, perseverance, courage, and common sense.

ELIZUR WRIGHT.

For thee, my country, thee, do I perform
  Sternly, the duty of a man born free;
Heedless, though ass, and wolf, and venomous worm
  Shake ears and fangs, with brandished bray at me.
ELLIOT.

ELIZUR WRIGHT is the translator of La Fontaine's Fables, and the editor of the Commonwealth. Mr. Wright is an original and subtle writer, has great power of analysis, and often flings the golden light of a vivid imagination over the productions of his pen. He may be styled the prince of paragraphists, and yet he often is as unidiomatic, angular and jargonic as Carlyle. Common objects and hackneyed subjects, viewed through the kaleidoscope of his fancy, have a charm which attract the attention of persons competent to appreciate his thoughts and illustrations. He usually writes on practical questions and every-day transactions, and in his peculiar way endeavors to remove evils, correct abuses, expose hypocrisy, denounce cant, condemn bigotry, and enforce the principles of universal freedom in church and state. When he assails a public man who has not been faithful in the discharge of his duty, he reminds one of the Rev. Sydney Smith, who had expended a great deal of elaborate censure on an English minister. Said he—"I do not attack him for the love of glory, but from the love of utility, as a burgomaster hunts a rat in a Dutch dyke, for fear it should flood a province."

Few men exhibit more versatility of talent than Mr. Wright. He can translate a French fable, write a popular song, originate a love story, dash off a leader for a newspaper, prepare an essay for a review, or rise up and make a speech, at short notice. Examine his spicy and spirited sheet, and you will see that it scolds like a cynic, reasons like a logician, while it glows with eloquence and gleams with poetry, and looks like a pretty woman in a fit of passion on a washing-day — scolding and slapping the little "brats" about her.

Mr. Wright sympathizes with the spirit of reform, which is now moving on the mighty deep of intellect; but he is so paradoxical at times, it is difficult to define his position. He looks upon black coats and white neck-cloths with suspicion, and is apt to crow whilst he chronicles defections in the church. He is an ordinary speaker, and never could attract much notice in the forum. His voice is weak, utterance slow, manner unattractive, but his matter is original and startling. He appeals to the people to look beyond their larders and their libraries, their farms and their factories, to gaze up higher than the steeples of their churches. He divides society into mice, owls, eagles, men, angels, and gods.

Our subject is a domestic man — a kind of utopian utilitarian. Few women can beat him at sweeping the floor, making the bed, or dressing a baby. At home, he is often up to his elbows in the kneading-trough and wash-tub. It is quite common to see him write with one hand and rock the cradle with the other. There are not many families in New England under better management than his. The oldest boy, who is now in his teens, is a famous and skilful teacher of music.

Mr. Wright has just passed the meridian of life; is a

small, thin man, of the nervous-bilious temperament; face strongly marked, indicating unbending endurance, unfaltering energy, and transparent honesty of purpose; head large, especially in the region of the reflective faculties. I should think benevolence, ideality, comparison, causality, combativeness, and philoprogenitiveness the most prominently developed organs. His editorials are quoted extensively in every part of the land. Eloquent extracts might be taken from the columns of his paper, and made into a saleable book. His sparkling sentiments, comical illustrations, witty conceits, droll humor and pat quotations are mixed up with theology, philosophy and science.

In a word, Mr. Wright is a scholar, a poet, a *genius;* he is obstinately independent, indignantly in earnest, and unmercifully severe. Notwithstanding all this, he would make a good conductor, if he had not so many cars attached to his engine.

JOHN M. SPEAR.

THERE are but few of the unfortunate inmates of the houses of correction, the jails and the prisons in New-England, who can with propriety say to JOHN M. SPEAR, "I was sick and in prison, and ye visited me not." He devotes himself almost entirely to the welfare of that neglected class of our fellow men, whose accidents and crimes have deprived them of the privileges which are the birthright of a free people. The poor prisoner, clad in the dress of a convict, was doomed to toil at the loom, the crank, the forge, the bench and the wheel, and pass through the same routine until death or the turnkey came to his relief, and apparently no one cared for his soul or his body. Sometimes the innocent suffered with the guilty, and often the guilty were punished beyond their deserts. But the sun of the nineteenth century now illuminates the moral heavens, and as the natural sun shines on the evil and the good, even so do the golden rays of this glorious luminary shine through the grated window of the prisoner's cell, and the true light reveals the fact that the convict stained with sin and harnessed with iron, is our brother. He has been badly educated, or temptations that might have overcome the Pharisee that scorns him, have proved his ruin ; or he has inherited from his parents a bad organization of brain ; or he has voluntarily surrendered himself into the hands of the evil one; or evil communications have corrupted his good manners. Although a criminal he is an object of commiseration.

Mr. Spear not only sympathizes with these violators and victims of the law, but he gives them good moral lessons. When they are arrested, he flies to their assistance,— procures counsel, or pleads their case himself. If they are found guilty, he labors to mitigate their punishment, petitions for pardons, and obtains employment for them when their term of imprisonment expires. His pen and purse, his tongue and time are given freely, cheerfully, constantly, to this work of righteousness. Carlyle would call Mr. Spear a rose-water reformer, a pink-and-senna philanthropist, a benevolent Bedlamite,— but he is really the Howard of America. He has travelled hundreds of miles, collected thousands of dollars, delivered scores of speeches, and written volumes of pages, to defend the prisoner. He has shielded the innocent from impending punishment, and alleviated and abbreviated the sufferings of the guilty, by bringing to light palliating circumstances that would have been buried in darkness. During the session of the Police Court, he may be found among the lawyers and reporters, prepared to assist the unfortunate and the guilty. He is an out-and-out reformer, and is not afraid to assail any form of evil, however large its bulk or hideous its horns. He is a sensible speaker, but not an attractive one; a calm reasoner, but not an eloquent one. In a word, he is a plain, practical, every-day sort of a man, whose look and manner convinces one of his sincerity.

Not unfrequently Mr. Spear starts off from the city into the country, without knowing beforehand where his tour will terminate. He travels under the hallucination that an invisible and spiritual agency is directing him to a destination where his services are needed. He is a tall, lean, boney man, with a black wig, a sallow skin, and a mouthful of large teeth. He wears a "can-I-help-you?" sort of a look, and speaks so gently and moderately, the listener, if ever so much excited before, becomes calm and feels at home, as in the presence of a friend and a brother. He is a Universalist minister, a temperance lecturer, an abolition promoter, an anti-hanging, anti-war advocate. His brother Charles is just like him, and is the editor of the *Prisoner's Friend*, a magazine, ably conducted. These brothers are as much alike as the Siamese twins.

JOHN AUGUSTUS.

John Augustus is the drunkard's friend. Most of his time is spent in the Police Court. When the unhappy disciples of Bacchus are brought into court, charged with drunkenness, they are usually fined two dollars and costs — the whole sum amounting to five dollars. It seldom happens that a common street-drunkard can raise that amount of money immediately after a "spree," and to prevent his being sent to the House of Correction, where he would be divorced from his friends and disgraced in his own estimation, this noble philanthropist steps forward with the funds in one hand and the pledge in the other, and in many instances succeeds in restoring the man to his family, and restraining him from the use of strong drink during the remainder of his life.

Mr. Augustus is an ordinary looking man. His hair, which is now quite grey, hangs like a mop over his forehead, as though he determined the organ of benevolence, like many of his kind deeds, should remain unseen. When he goes into court, his face looks as though he had died during the night, and had been galvanized into life before he got up in the morning. His saffron-colored skin is covered with wrinkles, from the tip of his chin to the top of his forehead. In that respect he is the most *remarkable* man I ever saw.

He is nervous and fidgety, when opposed. His labors of love are appreciated by some of the disinterested philanthropists of Boston, and they contribute magnanimously to sustain him. More than half the sum expended by him, in paying fines for drunkenness, is refunded by the parties who have been benefitted by his generosity. Mr. Augustus makes no pompous display, no noisy parade, about this matter; but day after day, and year after year, he visits the court and spends his time in watching over the welfare of the down-fallen and degraded.

Mr. Augustus is a good man, whose heart is as large as his head. He is far above mediocrity, in point of "good feeling." The "prisoner's friend" and the "drunkard's friend" are both poor men, but they are the unfaltering defenders of the humble and the despised, and on the great day of account many will rise up and call them blessed!

FATHER TAYLOR.

Such vast impressions did his sermons make,
He always kept his flock awake. DR. WOLCOTT.

I venerate the man whose heart is warm,
Whose hands are pure, whose doctrines and whose life
Coincident, exhibit lucid proof
That he is honest in the sacred cause. COWPER.

ONE Sunday morning I went to the Sailors' Chapel in Boston, to see and hear the far-famed mariner's preacher, Father Taylor. He was reading the familiar hymn which commences with the well-known lines, "Come, thou fount of every blessing," when I entered the house of worship. The choir wedded the words to music — the Divine blessing was invoked — a chapter was read — and then the sixteenth verse of the third chapter of Colossians was selected as the basis of the discourse. The striking peculiarities of the eccentric and celebrated preacher cannot fail to attract the attention of the seamen and landsmen who attend his church. He rises clumsily from the sofa in the pulpit, and puts his fore-finger on the text as though he anticipated the danger of losing it, or was determined to stick to it. After reading it distinctly and deliberately, he is pretty sure to raise the spectacles from his eyes and let them rest over the organs of causality.

Father Taylor does not ape the clerical stiffness which so ill-becomes those who strive to make up in dignity what they lack in devotion and intellect. When he walks the pulpit floor, like a caged lion, or pounds the desk with his fists, there seems to be, and doubtless is, honesty in his zeal. When he distorts his weather-beaten face, and swings his out-stretched arms about him, and shakes his lean fingers in the faces of his hearers, we see that he has in him the elements of a good actor. He is an odd genius, and I have no hesitation in affirming that he will utter more wise sayings and more sayings that are otherwise, in a single sermon, than any other man in Massachusetts. Not unfrequently he mixes his pathos and humor so evenly, the listener knows not whether to laugh or weep. One minute he appeals to Heaven, in a strain of sublimity that excites your admiration and astonishment; and the next moment he appeals to Mr. Foster, or some other member of his congregation, in a style not comporting with the idea most men have, of the dignity of the pulpit. Now, with compressed lips, grating teeth and flashing eyes, he denounces some vice or some heresy, in words steeped in a solution of brimstone; and then, with a smiling countenance, upturned eyes aud outspread hands, he lavishes encomiums on hope, faith, love, virtue, piety. Now he pours out a torrent of adjectives, as though he resolved to exhaust the vocabulary; then follows a stream of nouns, from his unfailing Cochituate of language. His sermons are ornamented with gems of poetry.

The following extracts from the sermon I heard a week or two since, will give the reader a tolerable idea of his matter;—his manner is unreportable, for he is the Booth of the Boston pulpit. "Some men," said he, "will lie for a glass of grog, and some women will lie for a cup of tea. If God respects some sinners more than others, there will be a back hole in hell for liars." "Who are so low, vile, mean, hateful, as the wholesale dealers and the retail pedlars in lies?" He prefaced a quotation from Proverbs with these words: "Solomon was a wise old fellow, although he had strange notions about some things." Speaking of back-sliders, he observed: "They slide by moonshining and deceiving themselves." He ridiculed, with bitter severity, the Oratorios of the present day; said that "profane lips dared to imitate the groans of Christ upon the cross. Infidels, with instruments of music, endeavoring to show the sufferings of the Saviour in the garden—the driving of the nails, the dripping of the blood upon the accursed tree—and they mimicked the blast of the angel's trumpet." It was an eloquent and just rebuke to those who trifle with sacred things.

Father Taylor is a plain-looking man, and his bronzed face is strongly marked. He is now in the sunset of life, and his head is thickly sprinkled with grey hairs. When excited, his voice is harsh, and conveys the impression to the mind, that the "man behind it" hates the Devil more than he loves Jesus. He is volcanic, and is often guided more by impulse than by intellect. Although he is in the autumn of his years, he can perform more service, endure more hardship, and preach better sermons, than half the young preachers of the present day.

ELIHU BURRITT.

"Our country is the world; our countrymen are all mankind."—ANON.

A SHORT time ago the friends of peace called a meeting at the Park Street Church, for the purpose of appointing delegates to attend the World's Peace Convention, on the banks of the Maine. In consequence of the inclemency of the weather, and the un-business like manner in which the meeting was advertised, there were but few persons present; but the distinguished gentlemen who were called upon to address that audience might have consoled themselves with the reflection that what their assembly lacked in number it made up in talent, learning, influence, and moral worth.

The chief object of attraction, at this meeting, was Elihu Burritt, the "learned blacksmith." He sat on the first seat opposite the pulpit, with his back toward the audience, his head resting on his hand, and his eyes closed most of the time, during the delivery of the speeches. Thomas Drew, Jr., immortalized as Burritt's "blower and striker" at the forge and anvil of reform, was busy with pencil and paper, in one of the side pews. The hearers waited peaceably but impatiently for Mr. Burritt to take the rostrum, and when it was announced that he would speak, every countenance became radiant with joyful anticipation. Mr. Burritt arose in a quiet, unpretending manner, and modestly responded to the invitation to speak. He stood on the top stair of the pulpit, and at first seemed to shrink back bashfully from the gaze of the upturned faces before him. Although he is no coward, I have no doubt his heart beat as though it would batter a breach through its tenement when he first unsealed his lips in the presence of that assembly. In fact, the contour of his face, and the tones of his voice, are the tell-tales which publish his lack of self-conceit.

Mr. Burritt is now in the meridian of his manhood, but his premature baldness is his apology for wearing a wig. He has a towering forehead, but, owing to the large development of the perceptive faculties, it appears to retreat. I think his eyes are blue, when they do not blaze. His face indicates perseverance that will not falter, and integrity that will not disappoint. He speaks slowly, distinctly, and forcibly, without ever uttering a foolish thing. He has a peculiarity of tone which is unreportable, but which tells with thrilling effect on the hearts of his hearers, when he enters earnestly into the subject he discusses. All who have heard him must acknowledge that his matter is as full of thought as an egg is of meat. He employs facts and statistics in his speeches and editorials, but they have the varied beauty of the rainbow, and the golden glow of sunlight, when viewed through the prism of his rich imagination.

The following extract from the London edition of the little volume entitled "*Sparks from the Anvil,*" will give the reader an idea of Mr. Burritt's style of writing. In an article on temperance, he alludes to the history of a distinguished statesman who had been snatched as a brand from the liquid burning: — "And he was found, with all the resuscitated vigor of his talents, *exhuming*, as it were, his fellow beings, who, like him, had been buried before they were dead. Massachusetts welcomed him back to her embrace with emotions of maternal joy, and invited the returning pleiad to resume his rank among the stars of her crown. The doors of her halls and churches were thrown open to the newly-returning prodigal, and many were touched to life and salvation, at the burning eloquence which fell from his lips. Sister states heard of this new Luther in temperance, and he obeyed their call. He stood up in their cities like Paul in the midst of Mars Hill, and, with an eloquence approaching inspiration, set forth the strange doctrine of total abstinence." That man, unfortunately, was led astray by fiends in human form, but a band of Washingtonians persuaded him to sign the pledge once more, and this time it was an unviolated policy of insurance against the fires of destruction. He concluded that graphic sketch in the following words: — "That man is again a giant, and he is abroad; look out for him! Like Samson, he is feeling for the pillars of the temple of Bacchus, and he will ere long revenge the loss of his locks by a mighty overthrow of that doomed edifice."

It affords the writer no small degree of pleasure to lift up the curtain which hangs between the past and the present, and look back to the time when the now eminent champion of peace first put on his paper cap and leather apron, and made the forge blaze and the hammer ring. He did not dream, then, that he one day would "beat swords into plough-shares and spears into pruning-hooks." His friends did not at that time give him credit for any striking manifestations of genius. To use his own words, he was a "plodding, patient, persevering" lad, gathering by "the process of accretion, which builds the ant-heap, particle by particle, thought by thought, fact by fact." In this way he worked and studied, night by night, for years, with "blistered hands and brightening hope," at lessons which have made him shine a star of the first magnitude in the firmament of fame.

In the Summer of 1838, Governor Everett, of Massachusetts, in an address to an association of mechanics in Boston, took occasion to mention that a blacksmith of that State had, by his unaided industry, made himself acquainted with *fifty languages!* Prior to this announcement, Mr. Burritt had lived in obscurity, and the fame of his acquirements did not extend beyond the smoke of his work-shop. When Mr. Nelson called on Mr. B. at Worcester, he found him at his anvil. When told what the Governor had reported respecting him, he modestly replied that the Governor had done him more than justice. It was true, he said, that he could read about fifty languages, but he had not studied them all critically. Yankee curiosity had induced him to look at the Latin Grammar; he became interested in it, and persevered, and finally acquired a thorough knowledge of that language. He then studied the Greek with equal care. An acquaintance with these languages had enabled him to read, with equal facility, the Italian, the French, the Spanish, and the Portuguese. The Russian, to which he was then devoting his odd moments, he said, was the most difficult of any he had undertaken. He went to Worcester to secure the advantages of an antiquarian library, to which the trustees allowed him free access. He spent eight hours at the forge, eight hours in the library, and the remaining eight hours of each day in recreation and rest. After he had studied Hebrew, and made himself acquainted with its cognate languages—the Syraic, Chaldaic, Arabic, Samaritan, Ethiopic, &c., he turned his attention to the languages of Europe, and studied French, Spanish, Italian, and German, under native teachers. He then pursued the Portuguese,

Flemish, Danish, Swedish, Norwegian, Icelandic, Welsh, Gælic, Celtic, &c.

It is somewhat remarkable that a man who has devoted so much of his time to the acquisition of languages that he is a living portable polyglott, should have such mighty mathematical powers. Figures tumble from his pen like seeds from a sack when the string is untwined from its throat. There are but few men of past or present times, that can excel him in description. Take the following graphic sketch of the iron horse, as a specimen of his skill in that department of literature: —

"I love to see one of these creatures, with sinews of brass and muscles of iron, strut forth from his smoky stable, and saluting the long train of cars with a dozen sonorous puffs from his iron nostrils, fall back gently into his harness. There he stands, champing and foaming upon the iron track, his great heart a furnace of glowing coals, his lymphatic blood is boiling in his veins, the strength of a thousand horses is nerving his sinews — he pants to be gone. He would 'snake' St. Peter's across the desert of Sahara, if he could be fairly hitched to it; but there is a little, sober-eyed, tobacco-chewing man in the saddle, who holds him in with one finger, and can take away his breath in a moment, should he grow restive or vicious. I am always deeply interested in this man, for, begrimed as he may be with coal, diluted in oil and steam, I regard him as the genius of the whole machinery, as the physical mind of that huge steam-horse."

Mr. Burritt believes that God has made of one blood all the nations of the earth, and he aims to unite them by the fraternal chain of brotherhood. He looks upon war as an inexcusable evil, and labors manfully for its extirpation. He would dismantle the arsenal, disband the army, spike the cannon, and reforge the cutlass; he would take our ships of war and "lade them down to the water's edge with food and covering for human beings." "The ballast should be round clams, or the real quahaugs, heavy as cast iron, and capital for roasting. Then he would build along up, filling every square inch with well-cured provisions. He would have a hogshead of bacon mounted into every port-hole, each of which should discharge fifty hams a minute, when the ship was brought into action; and the state-rooms should be filled with well-made garments, and the taut cordage and the long tapering spars should be festooned with boy's jackets and trousers. Then, when there should be no more room for another cod-fish or herring, or sprig of catnip, he would run up the white flag of peace. He would throw as many hams into the city in twenty-four hours as there were bomb-shells and cannon balls thrown into Keil by the besieging armies; he would barricade the low, narrow streets with loaves of bread; would throw up a breast-work, clear around the market-place, of barrels of flour, pork and beef, and in the middle raise a stack of salmon and cod-fish as large as a small Methodist meeting-house, with a steeple to it, and a bell in the steeple, and the bell should ring to all the city bells, and the city bells should ring to all the people to come to market and buy provisions, without money and without price. And white flags should every where wave in the breeze — on the vanes of steeples, on mast-heads, on flag-stones along the embattled walls, on the ends of willow sticks, borne by the romping, laughing, trooping children. All the blood-colored drapery of war should bow and blush before the stainless standard of peace, and generations of Anglo-Saxons should remember, with mutual felicitations, the conquest of the white flag, or the storming of Quebec."

Mr. Burritt has made his mark upon this age — a mark

which time will not erase. His society is courted by the great men of Europe and America. He quietly suggests a world's convention, and Senators, members of Parliament, Baronets, and crowned heads, hearken to his counsels. He is the same great and good man, whether in the smithy, talking with the hard-handed nailers, or in the magnificent forum, pleading for peace, in presence of the dignitaries of the land. He strives to smite off the clanking manacles from the uplifted hands of the bleeding slave, and to strike down the monster that wades in blood, and to build up the temple of universal peace, and to weld the world in an unbroken band of eternal brotherhood. He sees a spirit of selfishness abroad that would rob earth of its flowers and heaven of its lights, disinherit the angels, uncrown the Almighty, and sit upon the throne of the universe. So he has unfurled the white banner, and is now leading the crusaders of a good cause, to a battle where no blood will be shed, but where that evil, selfish spirit will be subdued, and peace shall triumph!

THURLOW WEED BROWN.

Thurlow Weed Brown is the editor and proprietor of the *Cayuga Chief*, a spicy and spirited sheet, published at Auburn, New York. Mr. Brown is one of the most noticeable men in the Empire State. He is remarkable for indomitable perseverance, steam-engine energy, and unfaltering courage. It is quite evident nature designed him for a leader, and he knows it; consequently, he not only commands the white-skins, but is "Chief of the Cayugas" also.

With no education but such as he picked up in a common school in the country, and no capital but that of brains and bones, he has established on a permanent basis one of the raciest reform journals in the realm of newspaperdom.

Although obstacles arose, like Alps on Alps before him, he bravely surmounted them, and pursued the uneven tenor of his way — bringing the timid time-servers and purse-proud pretenders who opposed him, to their marrow-bones.

He is rough and brilliant, like a rock abounding with diamonds; few men living have more power of origination, — and I hazard the assertion that he has written and spoken as many queer, witty, pithy, pointed and brilliant sentiments as any man of his age in his native State. It is generally acknowledged, by those who read his paper, that he commands a fascinating pen. Who ever saw a copy of the

Chief, out of his office, unfolded and unread? It is true that he is not always classically correct, in all he says and writes, and yet he makes fewer mistakes than many of our college-bred literati. The trees, with their branches pointing to the land of living spirits, and their roots pointing to the land of dead bodies, have been his teachers; and he has read the poetry of God in the country, written in letters of lilies, violets, and roses. Nature has spoken to him from beak and brook, and cloud and cataract, and he hearkened to her voice, and ever worships at her sylvan altar. There is the tinge of an opulent fancy glowing in his speeches and gleaming in his essays. Not long since, he awoke one fine morning and found himself famous, as an orator. His speeches consist of stirring appeals, strong arguments, and appropriate anecdotes — tied together with poetical sentiments. "If you disregard our petitions this year," said he, addressing the Legislature at Albany, "next year we will send petitions here with boots on." Did the limits of my book permit, I would furnish some specimens of his style. One thing I wish to notice: he is sometimes careless, and allows his pen to gallop, unbitted, over column after column of editorial matter; and he rarely, perhaps never, re-writes an article.

And I may say here, that his speeches are uneven. In one place he will deliver a thrilling speech — full of humor, wit, pathos, and argument — in another place he will be devoid of unction, and his address will be insipid as the essence of flat-irons. Such is apt to be the case with all men of true genius. Your mediocrity men are always the same; they never soar above their hats, and never dive below their boots.

Mr. Brown is now in the prime of life, — a man of ordinary stature and ordinary features. He has a large, well-balanced head, a long, rough, honest face, blue eyes, broad, high forehead, brown hair, and plenty of it — not only on his head but on his face, in the form of whiskers and goatee. In conversation, he is sociable, pleasant, gentle and modest, almost awkward — in consequence of his bashfulness. His pen is pugnacious, and while it pricks like the quill of a porcupine, it now and then drops a blot of egotism on the page it writes.

Mr. Brown will never die of the consumption, for the enlargement of his heart has caused an expansion of the chest. May he long live, to punish the wicked — whether they look from the gothic window of a wine-palace, or the grated window of a prison.

EDWARD BEECHER.

Oh, what is man, Great Maker of mankind!
That Thou to him so great respect dost bear,—
That Thou adorn'st him with so bright a mind,
Makest him a king, and e'en an angel's peer!

SIR JOHN DAVIES.

EDWARD BEECHER is a close thinker, a cogent reasoner, an impassioned speaker. His sermons are not elegant essays, got up for the entertainment of his hearers. They are not blank verse wire-drawn into very blank prose; not pearls and diamonds and precious stones, all stolen except the string that ties them together. They are true-blue, orthodox sermons, full of Beecher, truth, spirit, and scripture. They are living, breathing, talking sermons — famous for great thoughts and simple words.

Mr. Beecher is a fluent and forcible speaker, and makes use of the simplest (not always the purest) Saxon in his discourses. In his happiest mood his voice is often raised to a high pitch, and he soars with untiring wing higher, and higher still, and still higher, until his head is among the stars, and his face — like the countenance of Moses on the mountain — reflects the radiance of inspiration. He not unfrequently produces a thrilling effect by reiterated strokes, and by presenting epithet after epithet, figure after figure, fact after fact, argument after argument, appeal after appeal, which flow on like the waves of the sea, exciting the alarm of the unconverted who have spread their sail upon the waters of life, without provisions or pilot, and exciting the admiration of those who have, and those who *hope* they have fair prospects for reaching the haven of rest.

Mr. Beecher has studied mental philosophy, and is well versed in theology; has considerable knowledge of the ways of the world, for, unlike many of his cloth, he does not deem it a duty to shut himself up in his study continually, for fear of rendering himself "too common" to excite the wonder of the people on the Sabbath. There are some clergymen who keep themselves as wild as beasts are kept in a menagerie; you cannot see them without a ticket, and then you must keep at a respectable distance. Why, it is more difficult to obtain an interview with some ministers, than it is to have a *tête-à-tête* with the Pope of Rome! If Paul, with his hands hardened at tent-making, or Peter, fresh from his fishing-tackle, were to solicit an opportunity to preach in their pulpits, they would give Peter and Paul such a response as the Pharisees of old gave them. Dr. Beecher is not one of that class of spiritual teachers. You will see him in the streets, and at the exchange, in the reading-rooms, in the police court, at the public meetings in Faneuil Hall and Tremont Temple. He is a sociable, accessible, generous man, and capital company where he is sufficiently acquainted to "unbend the monkish brow." It is because he mingles with the people that he is in advance of many of his clerical brethren.

But Edward Beecher, like the rest of us poor mortals, has faults. He often seems to attempt to work up his feelings to a pitch of intense excitement. Under such circumstances there will be noise without eloquence, extreme gesture without extreme unction. In that way he exchanges the sublime for the sledge-hammer style. He has a good share of moral courage. Like his brother, the

"Thunderer" in Brooklyn, he assails with tongue and pen, from the pulpit and the press, the tergiversation, the coat-turning, the mouse-ing, the meanness of public men, who, for laurels or lucre, basely betray their country with a kiss.

The Brooklyn Beecher is almost constantly throwing shot and shell into the camp and court of the enemy. Some poor fool in his congregation became offended with him, the other day, because he publicly rebuked the recreancy of a prominent politician who recently betrayed his country, and put a crown of thorns on the bleeding brow of humanity. This nervous simpleton put down on paper the unpalatable sentiments he could not swallow, and had them published; and Sir Oracle, the editor, in all the pomp of pigmy grandeur, undertook to lecture H. W. Beecher on the duties of preachers! His labors were lost; for it does not run in the blood of the Beechers to be frightened at pop-guns in the arms of grasshoppers. Dr. Lyman Beecher, speaking of his two distinguished sons, said, Edward fires forty-pounders, and woe betide the man that he hits. Henry fires grape-shot, and kills the most men.

Edward Beecher is in the zenith of his manhood. He has used his brains more than he has his teeth, consequently his head looks older than his face. His hair is now turning grey; his forehead is broad and high, and indicates extraordinary intellectual power; his eyes are large and expressive, and burn like meteors, when he hides himself behind the cross and pleads earnestly for the welfare of men and the glory of God. He is one of the editors of the *Congregationalist*, a religious journal of great merit. He is also pastor of the church in Salem Street. At one period of his life, he was President of one of the Western colleges. He is a man of unimpeachable purity, has a highly cultivated

11

and strong mind, and is esteemed and honored in the walks of private and public life. Go and hear him, and he will prove, beyond doubt, that whatever is lovely in innocence, pure in virtue, good in morality, thrilling in eloquence, sublime in poetry, or holy in truth, may be found in the Bible.

HENRY WARD BEECHER.

HENRY WARD BEECHER is one of the boldest thinkers and bravest speakers in America. He not only wages war with unpopular vices, but has the courage to seize national evils by the throat; the mealy-mouthed Janus-faced politician, while *fishing for votes and catching suckers* in the ale-house, he holds up to everlasting indignation and contempt; the gambler, who in the great game of life "stakes his soul and lets the devil win it;" the lecherous libertine, whose look is lust, whose touch is pollution; the miser, who cheats the pale sewing girl, and defrauds his apprentice; the drunkard; the death-dealer; the oppressor, are all scourged by him; and every word he speaks is a blow; every blow inflicts a wound. Were he more ambitious than religious, he might employ the irreverent language of Pope, and say,

"Yes, I am proud to see
Men not afraid of God, afraid of me."

Mr. Beecher has studied the great folio of nature, and he can read men, whether they be bound in *boards, sheep, or calf.* He seems to be acquainted with the haunts and the habits, the slang and the signs of the great army of sinners. He never was a drunkard, but he speaks like one fresh from the *spirit land;* he never was a gambler, yet he speaks about high, low, jack and the game, as though he had studied the pack as well as THE BOOK; he never was a dandy, but he knows "how such die of a rose in aromatic pain;" he never was a demagogue, yet he knows how to unmask the demagogue. Mr. Beecher's invaluable lectures to young men comprise one of the richest galleries of word-painting to be found in the world of literature. Now he shews us an obese, greasy, wheezing, broken-down political hack; then a ripe, rosy, plump, luscious rascal, "whose spotted hide covers a tiger;" here we see a lank, lean miser, who would fling his last penny into his chest, sit upon the lid and swallow the key for fear he might lose it; there we see the drunkard, with his floating eyes and fiery face, &c., &c.

Mr. Beecher has a style of his own; it is more figurative than argumentative, more popular than classical. He has a fervid imagination, and although he seldom soars to the sublime, the beautiful is quite accessible to him; his humor is like a spirited colt—difficult to ride and hard at the mouth, sheering from the road frequently at the sight of its own shadow. He has great power of origination, and the skill to Beecherize what he borrows until it becomes his own. His mind is not a mint where every piece of metal bears the impression of a die, but a mine where gold can be obtained by the ingot; and he is a fool, and not an alchymist, who rejects it because there is some dross mixed with the precious ore.

He is a popular, but not an eloquent speaker; his matter is more entertaining than his manner. He is graphic, thrilling, earnest, forcible, but the burden of his reputation seems to encumber him. Could he drop the load and still retain the fame, as Christian did his bundle while he kept the roll, he would be eloquent as he is famous. When he goes from his closet to his pulpit, he has great power over the minds of his hearers; his sermons peninsulate the preacher with the congregation.

The subject of this sketch has more courage than most men of his cloth. While some of his cotemporaries made an auction block of the pulpit, and sold the Saviour in the person of the slave, for a few pieces of silver, or for fear of offending the "silver greys," he uncringingly denounced the damnable deed, and employed his prolific pen and tongue in defending the down-trodden and oppressed. His sermons and editorials are not still-born; they have open eyes and throbbing hearts, and they will continue to live and speak, when the wicked efforts of those who betray humanity will be forgotten; or if remembered, remembered with scorn.

Mr. Beecher is about thirty-five years of age, of common size and stature; has brown hair, blue eyes, pale complexion; a noble head, and thoughtful face. He puts on no awkward airs of assumed dignity, but is sociable, pleasant, and communicative. He is not only admired, but loved by the people of his charge. I will conclude this imperfect and hasty sketch, in the words of Hood, —

> "Thrice blessed is the man with whom
> The gracious prodigality of nature —
> The balm, the bliss, the beauty, and the bloom,
> The beauteous Providence in every feature —
> Recall the good Creator to his creature;
> Making all earth a fane, all heaven its dome!"

MASSACHUSETTS STATE OFFICIALS.

George S. Boutwell, Governor of the State, was born in Brookline, in 1818. Opened a shop in Groton, where he sold innumerable articles of domestic use. A real son of the Bay State — thrifty, prudent, sensible, shrewd, "knows-a-thing-or-two." Liked very much by his townsmen; sent to the Legislature, for the first time, in 1842, and soon made an impression. An able debater, skilful tactician, confidential leader of his party, (Democratic,) then in a minority. Was often appointed on some very responsible committees, and, in later years, on some of the most important commissions established by the Legislature.

In 1851, the Coalition made him Governor, the consideration being that Mr. Sumner should be the United States Senator. He has discharged his duties admirably. Affects popularity; seldom refuses to be present where invited, and is fond of military displays, agricultural fairs, educational demonstrations, &c. He is a temperance man; liberal in politics, though too cautious in speaking out his honest convictions; looks too much to his own popularity. It is said a portion of his inaugural address was examined by alarmed politicians. Nevertheless he has much merit as a citizen, a magistrate, and a man. He wants to go to the United

States Senate for the next six years, (but probably can't,) as he has signified he shall not again be a candidate for Governor. Has a firm reliance in the popular expression. He is in faith, a Unitarian; in works, a Utilitarian; in ideas, a Trinitarian.

AMASA WALKER, for the last and present year Secretary of the Commonwealth of Massachusetts, was born in Woodstock, Conn., in 1799. He first entered the Legislature in 1849. Now resides in North Brookfield. Was originally a Democrat, but early left that party and united with the Liberty party. In 1848 he was active in establishing the Free Soilers. Is a large boot manufacturer, in connection with his brother Freeman, and doing an immense business. Has no trouble in getting Southern custom, notwithstanding his Free Soilism; he knows that Southerners won 't go barefoot, (although they do not live in a free country,) for the sake of prejudice, and they can 't manufacture boots themselves.

Mr. Walker was formerly a resident of Boston, and active as a merchant. Deeply interested in all moral enterprises, he was in early life associated with a society of young men, who, by writing articles for the newspapers, public addresses, &c., *manufactured public opinion* to a degree that removed all booths from the Common, on election and other holidays, redeemed Beacon Hill from its then disgraceful reputation, and otherwise blessed the community. An early temperance advocate, a strong anti-slavery man, an eloquent peace advocate,—in fact, one of Elihu Burritt's life-guards; a friend of the abolition of the gallows—all from principle. Clear-headed, forcible, decided; a true republican, a real democrat, of and for the people. In 1849 he was sent as a Delegate to the World's Peace Convention, at Paris. As

Secretary of the Commonwealth, he never had a superior; everything is in No. 1 order. As a legislator, he is one of the ablest. He is the father of the Secret Ballot law, and also of many popular measures. In person, tall and thin.

Henry Wilson, now President of the Senate, is a native of the Granite State. He has seen life in various phases, having been School Teacher, Shoe Manufacturer, Member of the House of Representatives, Stump Speaker, State Senator, Delegate to the Whig National Convention, Chairman of the Free Soil State Committee, General of the Third Brigade, &c., &c. He is well skilled in Military and Political Tactics. As a speaker he succeeds admirably, because he does not attempt to pass for more than he is worth, and he exhibits that plain, practical common sense, which Massachusetts men never fail to appreciate. He has the faculty of dove-tailing one thought into another, and welding link after link into the chain of argument, with which he binds his opponent, which is quite alarming to political dandies.

Mr. Wilson is not more than forty years of age, and yet he has risen from humble life to an honored chair in the Senate Chamber; and this marvellous feat has been accomplished without the assistance of high social position, or lofty educational attainments. He has not yet attained his full growth, — there is a shining future before him.

He is a modest man and never forgets an old friend — never assumes an aristocratic or patronizing air. There is none of that lack-a-daisical insipidity or *miminee piminee* style of flash-and-go-out brilliancy, which too frequently characterize men who are suddenly elevated to posts of honor.

Mr. Wilson is a fresh, hearty man, in the zenith of life.

He is about five feet nine inches in height, well proportioned, and his frame indicates great vitality, strength, and endurance. His head is somewhat bald on the crown; his forehead white and broad; hair dark; eyes darker; cheeks ruddy; and lips red and full. He converses and presides well and impartially, without any swelling efforts at magisterial dignity. May his shadow never be less!

EDWARD L. KEYES, the "rabid" reformer, sits next to Judge Warren. He is the editor of the *Dedham Gazette*, one of the most spirited weeklies in the United States of America. Mr. Keyes has just risen, to explain and defend the Maine Law bill. He is a tall, thin man, with a pleasant face which is lit up with a pair of dark, dreamy eyes. I discovered a few threads of silver in his dark hair. How he stretches out his arms and shakes his lean fingers in the faces of his fellow Senators! He gives the Judge slap after slap in the face; — the recipient of the blows not relishing such a flagellation, whirls his chair around and turns his back upon the orator — but the lash of adders falls upon the shoulders of the victim, and vitriol is poured upon the red and gaping wounds.

Keyes is ferociously sarcastic; he leads the subject of his sarcasm like a lamb to the slaughter, and skins it alive, regardless of its imploring looks. See the Judge scowl, and twirl his spectacles, and shift his position; but Keyes keeps on, every word is a wasp buzzing in the ear and stinging to the quick; — there is electricity in his utterance. I am sorry that he now leaves the question before the Senate to defend the "Coalitionists." Such a course is untimely, and uncalled for, and almost unpardonable; the temperance question need not become a party question.

Mr. Keyes is a brilliant man — violent, vituperative, and

eloquent. His voice is deep and clear, and has that peculiar intonation which indicates that a man stands behind it. He flings the burning fluid of his indignation in every direction, and it burns in the hearts and on the faces of Senators and spectators, "one half of whom are ready to fight, and the other half ready to hurrah."

Charles H. Warren — the mouth-piece of the millionaires of Boston — has just arrived and taken his seat, on the left side of the President's chair. If he is a man of common calibre, then there is no truth in physiognomy or phrenology. The firm step, the compressed lip, denote obstinate energy; the towering forehead and beaming eyes indicate extraordinary force of intellect. The Judge is nearly sixty years of age, with a silver-grey head, bald on the crown; blue eyes, patrician mouth; is short, stout, and firmly built, dresses neatly, and looks like a "fine old English gentleman." He is an irresistible wag, and the fun he makes to match the arguments arrayed against his reprehensible course on the Liquor Bill, reminds one of the fiddling of Nero while Rome was on fire.

He brings down the house in roars of laughter, so as to startle the Sergeant-at-Arms, who looks as though he would be after the outsiders with a sharp stick, unless they governed their risible faculties. Still, he trembles while he rattles off his jokes, and looks like a man just taken from the whipping post, who cracks his *bon-mots* while the blood is streaming from his wounds. Doubtless his object is to divert the attention of the hearers, but it is evident he has no sympathy with the masses. He is elegant in his manner, and eloquent in his utterance — brimful and running over with genuine wit — dealing out his jokes as Sancho, in

Don Quixote, ladled out fat pullets and fat geese from the soup kettles, every time he made a dip.

Myron Lawrence is the oldest member and the largest man in the Senate. If size of body infallibly indicate equal mental and moral capacity, he is large enough to represent more than one constituency, for he is a man "with Atalantean shoulders fit to bear the weight of mightiest monarchies." His address is bold, frank, full of *bon hommie*, affording unmistakable evidence that his soul is not disproportioned to the magnitude of his physical organization. Speaking of himself, he says he has a hide like a rhinoceros; — if he really thinks so, he does not properly understand himself, for he is sensitive and loves the approval of his friends, as much as he dreads their displeasure. As a speaker he has but few equals in the Senate; and his speeches are more remarkable for depth than longitude. He is sociable, generous, and get-at-able; though strictly temperate, he loves the good things of this life. He has dark brown hair, half-shut eyes shaded with fat, a face plump and fair as the full moon, — is six feet tall, and weighs not less than three hundred pounds.

Anson Burlingame is probably not more than thirty years of age,— is about five feet eight inches in height, and fairly proportioned; has dark brown hair, usually brushed smooth as a bird's wing; — broad white forehead, indicating strength of intellect; — blue, magnetic eyes, and fair complexion. It is quite evident that he is fond of fame, and is extremely solicitous to secure the good opinion of his friends. Indeed, he is not reluctant to put himself to great inconvenience to accommodate others; — naturally gentle and generous, with impulse and intellect pretty evenly balanced.

He possesses the true *vivida vis* of eloquence,— and when he repents in sackcloth and ashes, over the unfortunate speech he made against the Maine Law, he will be a man the people will again delight to honor. His style is what may be termed poetical, and yet he displays a good degree of terseness and conciseness; is sparing of uniting particles and introductory phrases, and usually employs the simplest forms of construction. Knowing, as he does, that he is a universal favorite, he has taken the liberty to oppose the wishes and disappoint the expectations of his constituents, on the great question of the present age. Perhaps he and his historical friend may use the language of Hudibras:—

> "And have not two saints power to use
> A greater privilege than three Jews?"

Samuel E. Sewall is a descendant of one of the oldest families in Massachusetts. For a long time he has been an out-spoken, non-compromising abolitionist,—latterly associated with the Liberty and Free Soil parties. He is a man of upright intentions, generous sympathies, enlarged views, and unimpeachable purity of character. Bred to the profession of the law, and mingling in the busy scenes of life, he has been a close observer of men and measures. Though naturally quiet, modest, and unobtrusive, when aroused he defends himself and his friends with energy and power.

In the late effort to enforce the "infamous Fugitive Slave law," he was a prominent actor on the liberal side. Volunteering to act as counsel for the hunted bondman, on the memorable night Sims was arrested, some of our officials lodged him in the Watch-house for the time, an honor he may bequeath as an heirloom to his children's children. In person he is rather short and slight; hair quite grey; eyes blue; complexion fair. He wears his snow-white collar rolled over a thin cravat, and looks like a school-boy with his head powdered. As a speaker he is faulty; he talks in a low, quiet, deferential manner, as though he supposed his hearers knew more about the subject than he did himself, and has a habit of fumbling in his pockets, as though his ideas were in his purse. Notwithstanding all this awkwardness, the attentive listener will discover freshness of thought, soundness of logic, and purity of purpose. He is probably fifty years of age.

James T. Robinson was born in South Adams, Berkshire County, in 1822; educated at schools and academies, and graduated at Williams' College, in 1844. He had previously studied law in his father's office, (who is one of the ablest lawyers in Berkshire,) and on his graduation was admitted to the Berkshire bar, and went into partnership with his father, where he still remains. In '44, he stumped Berkshire for Henry Clay, in company with Rockwell, since honored by a seat in Congress. In 1848, left the Whigs and joined the Free Soilers, at great risk of business interest, popularity, &c., where he still remains.

Next to Burlingame, he is the youngest man at the Senate Board. Lightish complexion, greyish eyes, acquiline nose, thinnish in build. A graceful, earnest, whole-souled, nervous speaker. Reputed to be one of the most eloquent men in Berkshire, as he certainly is at the Board. A warm advocate of the Temperance and Anti-Slavery causes. He has rendered signal service for the new Liquor Bill, — by his exertions it was materially improved. He has rare talents, and is one of the most promising young men in the State, and a worthy follower of the eloquent Sumner.

Caleb W. Prouty is one of that rare class of legislators who seldom *talk*, but always rightly *vote*. He is a fit representative of the Old Plymouth Rock district—steadfast, frank, pure, principled. He is not a "brilliant" man; does not patter and spatter like many; but shines with a clear and constant light. Clearly understanding his subject, he lets his action speak louder than his words. Yet he is not reserved or distant, but cordial, fraternal and highly sympathetic. Few men, probably, have a larger number of personal friends among his townsmen and constituents than he.

Mr. Prouty is a native of Scituate; was born in 1810; has generally been a merchant or trader, yet never before the present year held a seat in the Legislature. He is one of the constants who are always in their seats. He voted, recently, on every proposition affecting the new liquor law, and what cannot be said of all the Senators, never voted wrong, in my judgment. As a member of an important committee, having in charge one of the great interests of the State, he has rendered signal service.

Mr. P. is of good build; open, pleasant face, set off with bright blue eyes. His hair is brown, rather thin, and stands up from a well-developed forehead. He dresses like a substantial man, rather than as a foppish one. He is active as a temperance man and Free Soil Abolitionist. In faith he is a Unitarian.

Charles T. Russell is an intellectual looking man, of the nervous temperament, has a pale, thin face, wears spectacles, and has made a spectacle of himself, by his hide-and-go-seek course on the Liquor Bill. He professes to be devout; pretends to be a friend to the cause he stabbed in the house of its friends, speaks freely and frequently, although he does not say much. Walks as though self-esteem had some influence over his heels and his hands. He is occasionally eloquent, and can reason when he takes the trouble to think before he speaks; has a good mind, a good education and generous impulses, but he lacks the courage to follow his convictions. He has not a very agreeable voice, and has the bad habit of emphasizing the most unimportant words; nevertheless, is urbane, pleasant and sociable; —

> "Tis with our judgment as our watches, none
> Go just alike, yet each believes his own."

Thomas G. Cary is a tall, spare gentleman, of elderly years, with curly, silver hair, long pale face, blue eyes, and a well-developed forehead. He is polite, pleasant, and conciliatory, squeamishly particular in matters of dress and address. Wishes to suit all people generally, and his own clique in particular. It is evident he has looked at only one side, and that the wrong side, of the subject of temperance. He is a calm, cool, moderate speaker; seldom soars to the realm of eloquence; never sinks into the unbridged gulf of vulgar and personal abuse. He never spins out long-winded, flimsy speeches; never wearies the listener with antithetical sentences; but generally gives you the point-blank truth, in the plainest and purest Saxon.

Christopher A. Church is a tall, agreeable man, with bright eyes, sharp, thin face; he is about forty years of age, speaks fluently and distinctly, without wasting words; he is sound on moral questions, and highly esteemed for his social qualities and amiable disposition. His Maine Law speech proves him to be no common thinker. He is engaged in mercantile pursuits, and much esteemed by his townsmen.

George H. Kuhn, of the Suffolk delegation, is one of the most useful Senators. As chairman of the important Committee on Mercantile Affairs and Insurance, he is hard-working, faithful, and expeditious, yet not slovenly. His labors are most complete. Without exception, I am told, he personally drafts more bills and resolves than any other member. He is a Boston man, by birth and residence; born in 1795; entered the Legislature in 1846; largely interested in the Western Railroad, of which he is one of the Directors. A little, sprightly, pleasant, bald, spectacled, polite man, whom every one respects. Does not speak often.

Charles C. Hazewell is a Rhode Islander by birth, and a type-setter by profession; and though entitled to the "Hon." from his position, finds more acceptable homage when addressed as a "jour. printer." He was born in 1815, entered the Legislature for the first time the present year, and resides in the pretty town of Concord. He is of good size, full forehead, bright eyes, white, transparent face, which shows every thought; wears silver-bowed spectacles. As a reader of history, but more particularly as a rememberer of it, he probably has not his superior. He lends a charm to any debate when he brings this vast knowledge into requisition. A most industrious man and cordial companion, though quickly excited at a supposed affront. Has edited innumerable papers, and written many of the ablest reviews which have appeared in print. He is a determined opponent of the Maine liquor law, but a frank and honest one. At present he is the political editor of the *Boston Times*.

John S. C. Knowlton, Freeman Walker, (brother of Amasa,) and Moses Wood, of the Worcester delegation, are substantial, talented, and influential members, though they talk but little. They are fit representatives of the intelligence and worth of the "heart of the Commonwealth,"—prompt in their places, and faithful in their duties.

WHITING GRISWOLD is the picture of health, ease, and good nature; yet his full forehead, and bright dark eyes, denote considerable intellectual power. In personal appearance he makes one think of the well-to-do country landlord, whose cordial welcome guarantees a loaded board, clean bed, and the best of care. He is not far from forty years old, rotund person, wears a blue coat with bright buttons, has a rosy cheek, and the most candid address. He is the sole representative of Franklin County, in the valley of the Connecticut, (of which he is a native,) is now regarded as one of the ablest leaders of the Democratic party in the State. As a speaker, he is sound, clear, thorough, well-informed, and though not a brilliant, is a very interesting debater. When roused to vindicate himself, or measures, or party, there is no half-way work with him. His dignified, calm utterance has great power. It needs but few words from him to make all the wit and facetiousness of Judge Warren appear the most contemptible twaddle. Mr. Griswold is a lawyer, and holds the responsible post of Chairman of the Judiciary Committee.

ZENAS BASSETT, of Barnstable, is a noble son of the sandy Cape. He is a native of the town and county he represents; followed the seas for many years, and settled down at last to receive the respect his many virtues command. He is tall, thick-set, with furrowed brow, grey hair, small, bright, laughing eyes, benevolent features; is sixty or more years of age; wears a dark blue frock-coat, and dark dress generally. Has the air of a substantial, sensible, generous, retired ship-master. One feels as though it would have been pleasant to sail in the same craft with him. An indefatigable worker; always present; seldom addresses the Board, but when he does, is plain and practical. Is a Whig of liberal views.

Edmund Kimball, of the Essex delegation, is a genial, pleasant, faithful legislator, prompt and able. Takes life as easily as he does an occasional pinch of snuff. Loves to crack a quiet joke with his neighbors or the Clerks. Lives up in Bradford, on the Merrimack, and is much esteemed as a citizen. Quite a temperance man, as well as Free Soiler. He is a morocco-dresser by trade, but there is no prunella in his composition.

Charles Hubbard is an artist of some celebrity. I am told he is a faithful committee-man, and invariably in his seat. He is interested in various public enterprises; somewhat, though creditably, particular to have everything under his charge well arranged and complete. He is a prominent citizen of Chelsea, and has served in various honorable capacities, but is as much identified with the interests of Boston as of the place of his residence.

Oliver Ames, Jr., is a silent member, but a practical worker and an eloquent voter; a man of middling stature, with small, sharp eyes. In business, he is a shovel maker, doing a large business, and is helping to dig the grave of the autocrat Alcohol. He is a man of liberal views, of Whig politics.

Charles W. Slack, Assistant Clerk of the Senate, is highly esteemed by members of all parties for his many excellent attributes, and is an universal favorite in the large circle of his acquaintance. As a friend, he is true as steel to the pole; genial as sunshine; generous to a fault; always polite and pleasant, and never fails to give a favorable interpretation to the words and deeds of others. He speaks easily and eloquently, but with too much constrained gesture; writes readily, forcibly, accurately. His stirring speeches and classical essays show that neither his sympathies nor attainments are meagre. Although much in public life, he is rather retiring in his nature; distrusts too much his own abilities; frank and open, and despises *shams*, whether of manners, measures or men. In person, he is of medium stature; light complexion; nervous-sanguine temperament; has blue eyes; light, silky hair; prominent forehead; thin, pale face; wears glasses; dresses neatly. He is a Boston boy, was brought up in the *Journal* office, and has been editorially connected with the *Excelsior* and *New-Englander*. Has rendered good service as a Temperance and Free Soil lecturer; and among his other accomplishments is a creditable phonographic reporter, and when desirous of it can have an enviable reputation thereby. A great lover of mirth, though he makes little himself.

Nathaniel P. Banks, Jr., Speaker of the House, is the man for the position he occupies — sharp, shrewd, impartial, polite, and thoroughly familiar with parliamentary usages. He knows every member at a moment's glance, and while he looks at the man (rising to speak) with one eye, he looks through him with the other, and announces his name, immediately and distinctly. Mr. Banks seldom makes a blunder, and he has tact and talent to conceal or correct many of the mistakes made by those whose bad manuscript and worse grammar would be a caution to the ghost of Lindley Murray, if read *verbatim et literatim et punctuatim*, from the Speaker's chair. He usually wears a brown frock-coat, buff vest, black stock. Mr. Banks has dark blue eyes, uncommonly expressive; a thin, pale, intellectual face; a plentiful supply of dark hair, (somewhat tinged with frost, although he is not yet forty years of age,) which is brushed so as to leave one temple bare, while it hangs down to the eye-brow on the other side.

He is a native of Waltham, born in 1816; first entered the Legislature in 1849; was elected Speaker of the House of Representatives in 1851, and re-elected in 1852 — probably one of the youngest presiding officers that ever graced the woolsack. He was brought up as a machinist and toiled with his hands, and exercised his brains by way of pastime. Self-educated. It is said that at one period he was an active fireman, and ran with the "machine," and, on holiday occasions, donned the red shirt, buff pants and leathern cap, — of late so distinguishing a mark of the brave and preëminently *cold-water* men. He subsequently left the work-bench for the office and green-bag, and was admitted to the Middlesex bar, where he has distinguished himself more by the faithfulness of his services to his clients than the receipt of an immensity of business. He has always been very popular in his native town, and could always be elected to represent it when every other man failed. Is of Democratic sympathies, and always has been, but inclines to liberal views. He is entitled to great credit for working his way so high in life, under adverse circumstances.

John Milton Earle is a fair specimen of a Massachusetts legislator, — honest, candid, and independent. He is a native of Leicester, born in 1794, and first entered the Legislature in 1845. For many years he has been editor of the *Massachusetts Spy*, the oldest newspaper in the State, and one of the most influential. Mr. Earle is a Friend or Quaker, wearing the broad-brimmed hat, (when not in his seat,) and straight-cut, standing-collared, brown coat, though in many respects not so rigid in his observance of the peculiarities of the sect as many of his brethren. In 1848, he united with the Free Soil party, and took with him his paper, which has a very large circulation among the farmers and thinking men of Worcester County, and the consequence was, the heart of the Commonwealth became the centre of the new political party, throwing the heaviest majorities for its candidates,— which position it retains to this day.

Mr. Earle is quite tall and spare; has a sharp, grey eye, though the general character of his face is mild and pleasant; his hair is straight, white and thin, as though it had withstood many storms, as indeed it has; his features are well wrinkled. He is clear-headed and sound on general questions. As a speaker, more interesting than brilliant, but his defect is that he talks too much. If his ammunition were saved for occasional battery-discharges, instead of constant pistol-snaps, more execution would be done. As a tactician, he is not the best — the truth being, he is too old and too candid for such nice work. Mr. Hopkins, this year, accomplishes in this respect much more successfully what Mr. Earle undertook last year. As a writer, Mr. Earle is terse, pungent, straight-forward, guided solely by principle, and ever alive to the necessities of the suffering. His age, character, and social position fully entitle him to the *soubriquet* of "Father Earle."

ERASTUS HOPKINS is considered the leader of the Free Soil wing of the Coalition, in the House. He was born at

Hadley, on the Connecticut, in 1810, and first entered the Legislature in 1841. In many particulars he is quite conservative and orthodox, like nearly all the dwellers in the Connecticut valley. By profession he is a clergyman of the Unitarian faith, though of late he has not preached, but obtained his subsistence by a connection with railroad enterprises. He is a man of not very prepossessing appearance, being sallow in complexion, of lightish-red hair and whiskers, and homely features. But when in conversation or debate, his whole appearance is changed — he becomes seemingly inspired. As an orator, he is bold and brilliant, appearing to best advantage, however, when favored with a little previous preparation. He was commissioned by the Governor, recently, to convey to Kossuth the official invitation to visit Massachusetts, and it is said his speech on the occasion of the interview even transcended in sublimity and grandeur that of the great Hungarian himself. Surely, it *reads* grandly. He is a ready manager, and nobly conducts the party in its parliamentary duties. His opponents find in him an able, yet courteous antagonist. A noble specimen of a Western Massachusetts man.

William Schouler, one of the leaders of the House, is a Scotchman by birth, and entered upon his career as a Legislator in 1844, in the thirtieth year of his age. He is a man of large sympathies, and though wedded to a political life, does not carry his party antipathies into the social or domestic circle. He is the principal editor of the *Atlas*, the leading Whig paper of New-England, if not of Boston, where Daniel Webster is supremely worshipped. But in this devotion the *Atlas* was always lukewarm. Mr. S. established his reputation as an editor, among the spindles of Lowell, and when he came to Boston, spit the *cotton* from his throat, and affected to stand on *free ground.*

He is a tall, thin man, with brown hair, blue eyes, and light complexion. At present noting, he has a rosy, healthy face, beaming with laughter and good nature. As a speaker, he is not very fluent, but generally interesting. His manners are rather awkward, as though he were so long he did not know how to care for his person. A man of great perseverance, but not always so consistent for the right in liberal politics, as some others. He is considered a good tactician, and has successfully carried through the House, heretofore, some important measures, solely by his persistence and skill. Is a great lover of festive gatherings, and presides admirably. He has held a commission in the Artillery service, has the title of Colonel, and is President of the Scots' Charitable Society. Is blessed with a lovely family, and resides in one of the prettiest cottages in East Boston, overlooking the protecting castles of the harbor.

Horace E. Smith is the champion of the Massachusetts Maine Law in the House. His opening speech was a masterly effort, and deserves to be written in letters of gold. While he sets a proper value on moral suasion, he advocates the use of coercive measures, when appeals and argument are powerless. He has studied the bill critically, and is thoroughly acquainted with all its provisions, and prepared to meet all the objections that may be raised against it. The great service he has rendered the good cause of temperance, will put a feather in his cap of which he and his descendants will be proud.

He is a pale, slender, graceful man, in the meridian of life; has a bold forehead, blue eyes, and brown hair; wears glasses; dresses neatly; speaks earnestly and distinctly, from a wise head and a warm heart. Success to him and his cause!

James S. Wiggin is the champion of the anti-temperance party, the leader of the opposition to the Maine Law, in the House. Although not a profound thinker, and quite an indifferent speaker, his perseverance and earnestness help to make up such deficiencies. In his recent defence of the rum-traffic, he was quite embarrassed, and acted so awkwardly that not a few of the grave faces present gleamed with fun, at his ludicrous blunders. His manuscript and his memory did not tally, for when he made an effort to speak extemporaneously, he soon found himself floundering in the mire,— and when he referred to what he had written, he made the discovery that he had taken the wrong sheet! Then, again, he was uncourteously chocked off, before he had time to wind up his speech. Notwithstanding all those difficulties, he gave one of the best speeches that have been made in either branch of the Legislature on that subject.

He is a tall, graceful, good-looking man, with sharp eyes, dark hair, and ruddy countenance. He is about thirty-five years of age; is engaged in mercantile pursuits, and would have to sacrifice what he calls property in the event of the passage of the law which he fights so ferociously. He is a keen man of business,— brave and energetic,— and will "stick at nothing" to defeat the bill he hates with perfect hatred.

James Small is the oldest member (not the oldest man) in the House. He is a plain, farmer-like looking person, nearly sixty years of age; has a broad chest, bronzed face, grey head, and bright eyes. Speaks out bluntly and fearlessly, with his spectacles in his hands; abounds in dry jokes; commands the respectful attention of the House. He hails from the "right arm of the Commonwealth."

Ensign H. Kellogg may be styled the leader of the Whig section of the House, having occupied formerly the Speaker's chair, and for the last two years, been his party's candidate for the same honor. He is a native of old Berkshire, was born in 1812, educated to the law, and made his *début* as a legislator in 1843. In the memorable contest which preceded the election of Charles Sumner to the National Senate, Mr. Kellogg most adroitly managed the Whig opposition, delaying action, and involving the Chair in a series of parliamentary intricacies, from which a man less skilful than Speaker Banks could hardly hope to be relieved. His former experience as the presiding officer, gives him superior advantages to most of his party for this sort of warfare.

Mr. Kellogg is an easy, clear, forcible debater, abounding in good humor, and occasionally keen retorts. His hits at opponents are oftentimes exceedingly clever. In person, he is of good stature, well built, with full face, bright grey eyes, dark hair "all up in a heap," wears black-bowed, lawyer-like spectacles, and has an inexpressible look of *bon hommie* and fun. I should judge he was considerable of a joker, as I know he is extremely sociable. A man of great force of character, and doubtless of high position hereafter, as of influence at present.

J. Thomas Stevenson is a Boston boy, Boston man, Boston merchant — in fact, Boston all over. Liberally educated, eloquent, able, social, generous, commanding, he truthfully represents the worth, wealth, intelligence and general excellence of the old Pilgrim city. He was born in 1807, received the advantages of the city schools and Harvard College, then entered upon mercantile pursuits, and soon reached the first place in his profession. In 1839 he first entered the Legislature, and more or less since has been identified with the career and fame of the State.

As a speaker, Mr. Stevenson has few superiors. His early liberal education, deepened and extended by an after life of active business habits, gives him the power to combine poetry and philosophy with great skill. He usually prepares his speeches beforehand, seldom making a set address without full-written notes in his pocket. His recent effort against the new liquor law, contains passages of portraiture of the evils of intemperance which cannot be exceeded in sublimity and choice expression by any words in our language. He is a Whig in politics, a warm admirer of Mr. Webster, and has a deep devotion to the interests of old Massachusetts. A benevolent, progressive sort of a man, but do n't want to go too fast; in this last respect his prudential fear too frequently checks the most worthy impulses. A warm friend, devoted parent, estimable citizen. Many noble enterprises have received his support, and numerous official stations have been honored by his connection with them.

He is now in the full maturity of manhood. Tall, prepossessing, olive complexion, keen grey eyes, well-turned features, and dark hair considerably frosted by age. He affects a brown or snuff-colored coat for ordinary wear, but otherwise dresses in dark-hued garments. Graceful in attitude, fluent in speech, and able in argument, he is a marked man in the lower branch.

Thomas E. Payson, of Rowley, Essex County, is a man of some character in the House. He is a stout, ruddy farmer, of great practical sense and shrewdness, and can break up land or sophistical reasoning with equal facility. He distinguished himself in 1850, by a speech against an agricultural college for instruction in farming on scientific principles, — a hobby some of the Boston amateur agriculturists have ridden nearly to death — which was *the* speech of the session. Clear, forcible, sensible, he upset and utterly routed the theorists, and killed the measure as dead as flies in a poison-dish, in Summer time. He is a native of Rowley, — thirty-nine years of age.

Otis P. Lord. — When I entered the House I heard the familiar voice of a gentleman from Salem, who speaks too frequently for his own fame, and the edification of his colleagues, to say nothing about the welfare of his constituents. It is quite evident he has a vast opinion of his own abilities, and if he is not the leader of the party to which he belongs, it is not owing to a superabundance of modesty on his part. He is a cautious man, and never ventures a step beyond the protecting wing of his party — a good party enough in the abstract, although it happens just now to be in a minority in Massachusetts. Mr. Lord is a man of respectable talents, and although he stammers and blusters, now and then, he says some very good things. He is in the prime of life, of common height and good build; dresses neatly, &c. His face is strongly marked, and indicates an arbitrary nature and aristocratic turn of mind. He looks like something between the silver grey and the blue stocking tribe. Has brown hair, blue eyes, broad forehead, and is of the sanguine-nervous temperament. He has in him the material for a good sea captain, or the leader of a legislative body. He is by profession a lawyer; a native of Ipswich, and made his legislative *début* in 1847.

Moses Kimball is one of the proprietors, and chief manager of the Boston Museum, a place of unexceptionable amusement. As a caterer for the gratification of the curious and wonder-loving public, he has few rivals and no superiors. He is a shrewd, keen man of business, who knows how to touch the public purse-strings. In politics, he is something of a cross between a Whig and a Native American; he is a man of fair talents, with unconquerable determination of purpose; sociable, generous, and good-natured; loves to see his neighbors prosper, providing their curiosity-shops are not too near his own. In matters of dress he is independent, foreswearing the use of dickeys. He is of medium stature, thick set, of sallow complexion, and has a full, fat face, indicative of good digestion; hair dark, eyes light, voice feminine.

It is quite evident he is ambitious of office, and good fortune has smiled propitiously upon him, for he has been a prominent member of the City Government, and is now an active Representative.

www.ingramcontent.com/pod-product-compliance
Lightning Source LLC
LaVergne TN
LVHW021405110826
845150LV00007B/1797

* 9 7 8 1 4 2 5 5 1 1 7 3 9 *